The Woodworker's Guide to
PRICING YOUR WORK

3RD EDITION

The Woodworker's Guide to
PRICING YOUR WORK
3RD EDITION

DAN RAMSEY

POPULAR WOODWORKING BOOKS
CINCINNATI, OHIO
www.popularwoodworking.com

READ THIS IMPORTANT SAFETY NOTICE

To prevent accidents, keep safety in mind while you work. Use the safety guards installed on power equipment; they are for your protection. When working on power equipment, keep fingers away from saw blades, wear safety goggles to prevent injuries from flying wood chips and sawdust, wear headphones to protect your hearing, and consider installing a dust vacuum to reduce the amount of airborne sawdust in your woodshop. Don't wear loose clothing, such as neckties or shirts with loose sleeves, or jewelry, such as rings, necklaces or bracelets, when working on power equipment. Tie back long hair to prevent it from getting caught in your equipment. People who are sensitive to certain chemicals should check the chemical content of any product before using it. The author and editors who compiled this book have tried to make the contents as accurate and correct as possible. Due to the variability of local conditions, construction materials, skill levels, etc., neither the author nor Popular Woodworking Books assumes any responsibility for any accidents, injuries, damages or other losses incurred resulting from the material presented in this book.

The Woodworker's Guide to Pricing Your Work: Third Edition.

Copyright 1995, 2001, 2005 by Dan Ramsey. Printed and bound in the United States of America. All rights reserved. No part of this book may be reproduced in any form or by any electronic or mechanical means including information storage and retrieval systems without permission in writing from the publisher, except by a reviewer, who may quote brief passages in a review. Published by Popular Woodworking Books, an imprint of F+W Publications, Inc., 4700 East Galbraith Road, Cincinnati, Ohio 45236. Third edition.

Other fine Popular Woodworking Books are available from your local bookstore or direct from the publisher. Visit the *Popular Woodworking* magazine Web site at www.popularwoodworking.com.

09 08 07 06 05   5 4 3 2 1

Library of Congress Cataloging-in-Publication Data

Ramsey, Dan (1945-)
    The woodworker's guide to pricing your work / Dan Ramsey.--3rd ed.
        p. cm.

    Includes index.

ISBN 1-55870-739-5 (alk. paper)
1. Woodwork--Prices. 2. Home-based businesses. I. Title: Pricing your work.
II. Title

TT180.R36 2005
684'.08'0688--dc22

2004051361

Acquisitions Editor: Jim Stack
Editor: Amy Hattersley
Cover Designer: Brian Roeth
Cover Photographer: Tim Grondin
Production Coordinator: Jennifer Wagner

fw
F·W PUBLICATIONS, INC.

For Dee and Toni Richards

Acknowledgements

Writing a book is a team effort. Thanks so much to the team who helped develop this book through three editions: Michael Carroll, business coach extraordinaire and owner of Mendocino Coast Furnituremakers; Jim Streeter of J.M. Streeter Woodworking; Rick Rochon of Olor Enterprises; Sharon Mast of The Myrtlewood Gallery; Jim Deardorff of Out of the Woods Furniture Co.; Vance Fortenberry of The Whittler; Dee Richards of East County Saw Shop; Jim Stack, Amy Hattersley, David Lewis and Brian Roeth of Popular Woodworking Books; A.J. Hamler, Ian Bowen, Thomas Clark and Dan MacAlpine of *Woodshop News*; Marilyn Stevens and Mary Jo DiAngelo of *The Crafts Report*; Edward F. Gallenstein of the National Wood Carvers Association's *Chip Chats*; Donna J. Pierpoint of *Fine Woodworking*; Helise Benjamin of the American Craft Association; and Lori Capps of the Business Development Center at Southwest Oregon Community College.

In addition, the author thanks the U.S. Small Business Administration, Office of Business Development; Service Corps of Retired Executives, Portland, Oregon, District Office; U.S. Department of Commerce, the Office of Business Liaison and the Minority Business Development Agency; Internal Revenue Service; and the staff of Communication Solutions.

Thanks, too, to the many magazines that inspire and serve woodworkers and craftspeople: *American Woodworker, Crafts, Crafts 'N' Things, Fine Woodworking, Popular Woodworking, The Crafts Report, Woodworker's Journal, Weekend Woodcrafts, Wood, Woodshop News, Woodwork, Woodworker, Workbench* and others.

Names, addresses, telephone numbers, Web addresses and related information are included in this book for the convenience of the reader and were current when this book was written. No endorsement is implied.

The author and publisher have used their best efforts in preparing this book, but make no warranty of any kind, expressed or implied, with regard to the instructions and suggestions contained in this book.

Foreward

BY MICHAEL CARROLL

Reviewing this text on pricing has brought back many memories of my 30 years of woodworking. For most of that time, I was an amateur, doing woodwork because I enjoyed it. I was making my living doing other things. Then, I was fortunate enough to study woodworking for two years with James Krenov. For the last nine years, I have been a professional woodworker and have sold my work into private collections both in the United States and Japan.

One thought I have is about being an amateur. In his book *The Fine Art of Cabinetmaking*, Jim Krenov speaks for the amateur in its literal sense (the word comes from the Latin *amore* "to love"): "those who love the material and the work of their craft more than anything else about it." Most of the professional woodworkers I know got into this field not because they expected to make a fortune, but because they love working with wood. In this sense, for many woodworkers, the distinction between amateur and professional disappears.

When I teach a class on business for woodworkers, by far the most troubling question is how does one make a living at woodworking, and the core of that problem is pricing.

In this book, Dan has done a thorough job of looking at the business of woodworking, not just for the professional, but for anyone who has occasion to sell his or her work. If one is trying to make a living, the lessons are essential. But even for the amateur or hobbyist, setting a fair value on your work should be important not just to support your hobby, but in putting value on Craft. Craft items today are a disappearing class. Mass production and cheap imports are leading people to forget the beauty and the artistry of woodcraft items.

If I have one message to reiterate from this book, it is to be unique. If you make a box or a turned bowl that looks just like someone else's box or turned bowl, who is going to care? Why bother and most importantly, why should a customer pay more than for a cheap mass-produced item? But if you develop your own style, and you achieve a reputation for making a unique craft item, your price and your ability to support yourself will increase.

Michael Carroll is a professional woodworker (Mendocino Coast Furntituremakers, www.mendocinofurniture.com) and business coach living on the Mendocino Coast in northern California.

Contents

CHAPTER ONE

The Craft of Pricing

CHAPTER TWO
Pricing Crafts and Folk Art

CHAPTER THREE
Pricing Woodcarving and Woodturning

CHAPTER SIX

Profitably Using Technology

APPENDIX

Useful Forms for Woodworkers

Introduction

Woodworking is a fun hobby. It can also be an expensive one. If you'd like to cover your woodworking expenses — and make a few extra dollars — without sacrificing your independence, *The Woodworker's Guide to Pricing Your Work, Third Edition*, by Dan Ramsey is for you. You'll learn how professionals in every field of woodworking set their prices and sell their products: crafts, folk art, carvings, turnings, furniture and cabinetry. You'll learn how to sell the value of your work to your customers so that the price is less important. You'll also learn how to increase your profits without sacrificing the quality of your work — or your enjoyment of woodworking. A new chapter has been added to this edition that explains how computers, the Internet and other technology can add profits.

Chapter one introduces you to the craft of pricing. Like any other craft, pricing has raw materials, tools, techniques and a finished product. This chapter introduces these components of pricing and illustrates each point so you can easily apply them to your woodworking craft. It covers estimating material costs, labor, overhead and profit. It also shows you how to sell the value of your work, how to negotiate and how to increase your prices. It even explains why prices are different from region to region — and how to benefit from it. The first chapter also includes forms and worksheets to help you price your woodworking.

Chapters two through four apply the basics of pricing to specific woodworking crafts: craft and folk art, woodcarving and woodturning, furniture and cabinetry. Each chapter applies the latest pricing rules to specific projects to illustrate how to price your woodworking. It covers costing materials, setting shop rates, estimating overhead and ensuring profit for a wide variety of wood crafts.

Chapter five offers proven methods of how to effectively market and profit from what you make. You will learn from the experiences of dozens of successful woodworkers. It covers record keeping, selling at craft shows and flea markets, consignment sales, mail-order sales, how to reduce material costs, upgrading tools and making your shop more efficient. It also includes advanced techniques for making your woodworking pay for itself: managing cash flow, building repeat business, getting valuable advice, paying taxes and much more.

Chapter six opens up the world of computers, the Internet and technology to the woodworker. It describes how to select computers and related hardware and how to find software that makes your job easier and your business more profitable. It shows the woodworker how to enhance craftsmanship by letting technology do the mundane work. Most important, it shows you how to take advantage of new technologies to work smarter, sell more and enhance your enjoyment of woodworking.

Throughout this book you'll find specific formulas, practical business practices and case histories, all explaining how to price your work in the most effective manner. The appendix includes valuable forms and worksheets that can easily be copied and imprinted with your woodworking business name to help you price and market your woodworking.

You may not necessarily want to turn woodworking into a money machine, but it would be nice to earn some income for your talents and skills while offering quality-crafted woodworking to others. By learning to price and sell some of your work you can enjoy woodworking even more.

The Woodworker's Guide to Pricing Your Work, Third Edition, is written not just for the amateur woodworker but also for the professional who wants to make more money at what he or she does. It includes numerous proven ideas from successful woodworkers on how to price, produce and profit from their part- or full-time business. This book incorporates common product-pricing methods with the experiences of numerous successful woodworking businesses.

The Woodworker's Guide to Pricing Your Work, Third Edition, is the first book attempting to give specific pricing information on a wide variety of woodworking products. It is comprehensive, but it will never be complete. Please share your pricing experiences and ideas with the author by writing to him in care of the publisher so that future editions will be even more helpful to fellow woodworkers. Write to:

Dan Ramsey, *The Woodworker's Guide to Pricing Your Work*
c/o Popular Woodworking Books
4700 East Galbraith Road
Cincinnati, OH 45236

Thank you and best wishes!

Dan Ramsey
Woodworker
Business adviser
Founder of the Fix-It Club (www.FixItClub.com)

ONE

The Craft
of
Pricing

How much should I charge for my woodworking? This is one of the most commonly asked questions from both new and experienced woodworkers. And it's a very important question. Though most woodworkers aren't looking to get rich with their hobby, they do want to pay for materials, buy additional equipment, repair current equipment, and have something to show for their time and skills.

This chapter introduces you to the craft of pricing your woodworking products. In it, you'll learn how all products — from soap to ships — are priced. You'll also learn how to sell the value of your woodworking. You'll discover tips on negotiating, selling to friends and raising your price.

Most important, you'll add a new skill to your toolbox: You'll learn how to offer greater value to your woodworking customers.

Making Money with Your Hobby

Maybe one of these situations has happened to you:
- Someone wants to buy your woodworking, but you don't know how much to charge.
- You can't afford to purchase expensive stock for your next project.
- You can't justify the cost of repairing your old jigsaw, but you can't bear to part with it either.
- You need additional income and would like to sell some of your woodworking.
- You want to retire soon and would like to develop an income from your woodworking to cover expenses and offer a profit.

Pricing your work can be one of the most frustrating components of woodworking — until you understand that pricing, like woodworking, is a combination of craft and art. The craft of pricing can be learned just as the crafts of wood selection,

assembly and finishing are learned. Art comes after years of applying craft until it is second nature.

Bill Jackson carved cowboys and other Western characters from local woods, selling them directly to people who stopped at his service station. He displayed them in the office window with the price written on a small sticker on the base of each piece. Bill priced the carvings at $10 each or three for $25, but sold very few. He didn't understand why so few sold, because he had put up to three hours of time into each carving, besides the cost of materials.

Then, from a business consultant, Bill learned the craft of pricing and marketing his carvings. Today, his carvings are sold in area gift shops for $100 to $175 each, with Bill getting half of that amount. Bill now carves full-time in his own shop and sells 15 to 20 carvings a week to a wholesaler who handles marketing and distribution. The wholesaler wants Bill to do more, but he's satisfied with his output and his income for now.

Intrinsic Value vs. Pricing

Why should you consider the craft of pricing? Doesn't art set its own intrinsic value and sell itself?

Craftsmanship is applying your knowledge, skills and creativity to tangible projects. Craftsmanship combines the natural beauty of wood with the symmetry of shapes into a beautifully turned and finished bowl. Craftsmanship brings art to life and gives it function.

Craftsmanship must reward both the receiver and the maker. Money is simply a way to exchange talents. An accountant exchanges her talents and training in finance for your talents and training in woodworking. Money is just the medium of exchange.

So the craft of pricing your woodworking is as important as other crafts you use. And while art sets its own value and sells itself, the craft of marketing must be applied to ensure that those who appreciate fine woodworking have the opportunity to purchase it. That's what this book is all about:

pricing and marketing your woodworking.

Think of it this way: If you spend money on it, it's a hobby. If you make money on it, it's a business.

The Basics of Pricing

You've stopped at a local hardware store for a new dado blade. A 7" adjustable carbide-tipped dado has a sign in front of it that says "$49.95." You think for a moment, "I paid $40 for my last adjustable dado and it lasted quite a while. I got a lot of use out of it; it was really useful when I built my shop shelves. I'll get it." You already know how to "price."

What Is Pricing?

Price is simply what you're willing to give up in exchange for what you want. You would not give up $1,000 for an adjustable dado blade, but it is worth about $50 to you. That $50 may have cost you a couple of hours of your time; you figure the dado blade will save you many times more than that. So you exchange the price (plus applicable state and local taxes, of course) in cash for what you want.

This process is repeated at the grocery store, the car lot and anywhere that you give someone money for what you want. It's much easier to give the store your money than to offer to come in and build some shelves for them. You exchange what you have (time and skills) for what you want (dado blade, groceries, car). Money is a convenient medium for the exchange. The next customer at the hardware store may be exchanging the equivalent of a half hour's time and skills for the blade — or six hours' time and skills. In each case, the hardware store gets the same amount of money. That's their price.

How Are Prices Set?

How did the hardware store set the price of the dado blade? The store or the manufacturer probably conducted some market research to determine the price at which people will exchange money for the blade while allowing a fair profit for both the manufacturer and the store.

Market research is a craft in itself. Basically, though, it answers four questions about pricing.

1. How much is the dado blade worth to the customer? That is, what is the value of the benefit that the dado blade gives to someone who buys it? If it saves the customer time, how much time and what is that time worth?

2. What will customers actually pay for a dado blade? This second question considers the customers' experiences in buying dado blades. Are most blades on the market priced above $100? Below $20? In the $30 to $60 range?

3. Can the manufacturer and retailer pay for costs and make a profit at that price? This is an important question. If the retailer cannot sell dado blades at more than $25, the price he must pay for them, he cannot pay for the cost of operating his store and will lose money on each sale.

4. Finally, can the retailer make more profit by selling a few dado blades at a higher price or more at a lower price? You see the answer to this question everywhere. Woodworking stores sell a few specialized blades at higher prices while discount stores sell hundreds of common blades at lower prices. Both profit, because some people shop for price alone while others shop for value.

Of course, you can't be like the man who had a sign on his whirligigs that read "$1,000 each." When asked if he sold any he said, "Not yet. But when I do, I'm going be rich!"

Types of Pricing

Pricing adjustable dado blades, industrial tools or automobiles is a complex process that requires the investment of hundreds of hours and many thousands of dollars. Pricing your woodworking is much easier, yet it applies many of the same rules and techniques.

Simplified Pricing

Most new woodworkers use the simplified pricing system. That is, they multiply the number of hours required to complete the job by a basic hourly rate, then add in the materials. For example, a lawn chair may take three hours to make. The woodworker multiplies three hours by, say, $15 an hour, then adds in the cost of materials: $14. The total comes to $59. That's the price.

This method of pricing has many problems. First, it doesn't pay you enough for your skills and your tools. Once you've deducted the cost of shop equipment, tool replacement, sharpening services and utilities, you're getting minimum wage. And you're still not earning any interest on the money you've invested in your equipment. At these prices, the first major power tool that goes down will take your wallet with it.

Sophisticated Pricing

Let's look at how successful businesses price their products and services.

The first step to pricing your woodworking is to determine what type of price you will set. Are you pricing wooden bowls that you will sell at craft shows (retail) or to a craft store (wholesale)? If you wholesale your products, what price do you suggest the retailer sell them at? A retailer is someone who sells a product to the ultimate or final consumer. The retail price is simply the price at which it is sold to the consumer. A wholesaler is someone who sells the product to the retailer at the whole-sale price. A manufacturer is someone who makes the product and sells it to the wholesaler, the retailer or directly to the consumer.

To set the price of your woodworking you need information about the cost of materials, the labor required to make the piece, the cost of overhead and the amount of profit you should reasonably expect. Let's look at each of these components briefly.

MATERIAL COST

Material cost is the cost of the materials used directly in the final product, such as wood, screws, machine nuts, tubing and paint in building whirligigs. Supplies such as sandpaper and saw blades are part of overhead, not material cost. However, the cost of picking up materials or having them shipped to you is a part of the cost of the materials rather than overhead. If it becomes part of the finished product, it is material; if not, it is overhead.

LABOR COST

Labor cost is the cost of effort needed to manufacture the woodworking product. Labor not directly applied to making the product is an overhead cost. Labor cost includes both the hourly wage and the cost of any employment taxes and fringe benefits packages. You'll learn how to set your labor costs in the form of a shop rate later in this chapter.

OVERHEAD COST

Overhead cost includes all costs other than direct material costs and direct labor. Overhead is the indirect cost of making your woodworking product. As noted earlier, the cost of sandpaper and cleanup time are overhead costs. Think of material and labor as direct costs — expenses that can be directly tied to the making of a specific woodworking product — and overhead as indirect costs or expenses that cannot be tied to a specific product. If you have purchased this book to make a profit with your woodworking — which I assume you have — the cost of the book is an indirect cost and can be deducted from your taxes as a legitimate business expense. It is a part of your overhead.

PROFIT

Profit is the amount of money you have left over once you've paid all the bills. Many woodworkers who have invested hundreds or thousands of dollars in their shops and their skills never consider that they should receive a return on that investment. They would never think of renting money to a bank interest-free, but will to their business. A fair profit is vital to the success of your woodworking enterprise. Without it, your woodworking business may not be here a year from now to serve new customers with great new products.

Pricing Categories

What pricing categories are most popular with consumers? Recently, *Woodshop News* conducted a survey of one hundred craft shops across the nation to determine what woodcraft products they buy, from whom, how they buy and how much they sell them for. More than half of the shops said their most popular price range for woodworking products is $25 to $75. Another 25 percent of the shops sold the majority of their woodcrafts in the $75 to $150 price range. Eighteen percent of the shops sold most of their products under $25, and another 6 percent sold the majority of their items at an average price of over $150.

Markup

One way of pricing your woodworking is called markup. Markup is a percentage of the materials cost that is added to cover labor and operating expenses. As an example, a cabinetmaker may add 100 percent of the cost of materials as the cost of labor, another 100 percent for the cost of the shop

(rent, tools, office supplies, etc.) and another 50 percent for profit. That's a total markup of 250 percent, or 2.5 times the materials cost. Here's the equation:

Cabinet Materials	$500.00
Markup ($500 x 2.50)	$1,250.00
Total Price	$1,750.00

Another way of looking at markup pricing is to establish a "rule of thumb." In the cabinetry example above, the rule of thumb developed is to price the job at 3.5 times the materials cost.

100% of Materials Cost
+ 250% Markup
350%, or 3.50, or 3.5

If the materials cost $500, the rule of thumb ($\times 3.5$) suggests a retail price of $1,750. Many successful woodworkers come up with such a rule of thumb that meets their needs. However, as you will see throughout this book, rules of thumb can lose you money and customers. I'll show you how to price smarter with just a little more effort.

Estimating Material Costs

As noted earlier, your material cost is the price you paid for any materials that are used in making your woodworking project. For woodturning, it is the blank. It is also the cost of getting the blank to your shop, such as shipping or freight charges or car mileage charges to pick it up. However, material cost does not include the cost of your lathe, sandpaper or related shop costs. These are considered "overhead" and will be covered in a moment.

Creative Woodcraft Inc.

Materials Use Record

123 Main Street, Yourtown USA 12345

Date May 7, 2005

Page 3   **of** 7

Type of Material: Walnut

Location : South wall racks

Size	Cost	How Used	Amt. Used	Value
3/4 x 2-3/4	$1.45	Johnson custom jewelry box - sides	12	$17.40
3/4 x 5-3/4	$2.10	Johnson custom jewelry box - top	3	$6.30
1/2 x 1-3/4	$0.85	Johnson custom jewelry box - trim	12	$10.20
			TOTAL	$33.90

Notes:

Figure 1-1. A Materials Use Record helps you determine the cost of specific materials and, in turn, helps you to price your woodworking more accurately. A blank form that you can reproduce and use is included in the appendix.

Record Keeping

How can you know how much a specific material costs? The large blank you purchased may have been sawn up into smaller blanks. The answer is that you keep good records. Figure 1-1 is a sample Materials Use Record. It gives you a place to record the actual costs of materials that you purchase and how you use them in your woodworking. You don't have to account for every fastener, but by keeping track of how you use your materials you will soon learn how much it costs — and be better able to price your woodworking.

As an example, suppose you build kitchen cabinets and have purchased 24 pairs of no-mortise hinges to get a discount on the price.

4 packs of 6 pairs hinges @ $15.95	$63.80
Shipping	$8.95
Total	$72.75
Cost per pair of hinges	$3.03125
Hinges used for Rogers' cabinet job	
10 pairs @ $3.03125	$30.31

This same principle can be applied to any type of woodworking. When you buy a piece of clear oak you record the total material cost, figure its cost by square foot or running foot, and keep track of its use. By keeping these records you can accurately estimate the cost of materials for a job in just a few minutes.

In some cases, costing materials can be more work than it's worth. You won't want to count each wood screw or bolt and add $0.001, as an example, for each one you use. Instead, you can estimate the number of units you will use on a "typical" project, figure the approximate cost of fasteners for the project, and record the cost in your pricing book. So, in estimating a future project, you add in that amount to cover fasteners. As your woodworking business grows and you're spending hundreds of dollars on fasteners, you can review your costs. But for now, an estimate will be sufficient.

When adding the cost of materials to a proposal, some woodworkers will quote material costs at retail prices that the customer would have to pay. Solid brass drawer knobs, for example, are quoted at $5.49 each even though the woodworker can purchase them at $4.12 each from his wholesaler. Shipping charges may or may not be added to this retail cost, depending on total shipping charges and the pricing policy of the woodworker.

Pricing Book

This is a good time to start your pricing book. It will be a place to record what you're learning about pricing your woodworking. It can be a loose-leaf three-ring binder, a bound record book, a card file, a manila folder or a computer spreadsheet program (see chapter six). In it you can include material worksheets, labor and overhead worksheets, estimate worksheets, and any pricing guidelines that you develop.

One more point: You may consider keeping all these records a waste of time. Actually, it's not. In fact, by learning how to price your woodworking through good records you'll reduce the time it takes to develop an accurate estimate. You'll also reduce the time you spend on unprofitable woodworking projects. You'll have more time for doing what you enjoy: making sawdust!

Estimating Labor

No two woodworkers work in the same way nor at the same speed. One may insist on using only hand tools. Another will build with the latest power tool using jigs for mass production. Skill levels and experience will also be different. Even so, accurate labor costs can be set by learning how you work.

Figure 1-2 is a typical Woodworker's Time Sheet. It offers an easy way to record your time so you can estimate the amount of time needed to do

Creative Woodcraft Inc.

Woodworker's Time Sheet

123 Main Street, Yourtown USA 12345

PERIOD END	MONTH	DAY	YEAR	NAME	TYPE OF WORK	
	10	22	2004	Bill Jones	Cabinetmaking	

TIME DISTRIBUTION FOR PERIOD

Description of Work	1	2	3	4	5	6	7	8	9	10	11	12	13	14	15		Total Hours
	16	17	18	19	20	21	22	23	24	25	26	27	28	29	30	31	
Measurement and design								2									2
	3								2								5
Layout and millwork			3	1					4	4							12
		4							2			4	4				14
Assembly								2			3	5					10
			4												5	3	12
Finishing			1	2										4			7
						4	5									4	10
Installation					4	5										6	15
	1						2	4									7
Holiday																	
Personal Ilness																	
Total Hours (incl. overtime)																	
Overtime																	

Total Hours | **99**

List of Expenses and Dollar Value (attach receipts)					Direct Hours	Indirect Hours
Description	$	Description	$			
		Total Expenses				

Figure 1-2. A Woodworker's Time Sheet will help you determine how much time is required for specific tasks, making it easier for you to profitably price your woodworking products. A blank form that you can reproduce and use is included in the appendix.

a specific project. The time sheet can be used chronologically, writing down the task description and time it took in the order in which it was done. Or you can keep track of your time on a chronological time sheet and then summarize time by task on a labor worksheet.

Using Worksheets

How you track your time depends on the type of tasks you perform, how long they take and how you feel about writing everything down. You certainly don't want to spend more time recording your activities than it takes to do them. Tasks can be summarized, such as: built 12" × 16" drawer with hardware, 1.2 hours.

What should you include on your labor worksheets? Any activities that are directly related to woodworking production; that is, record time needed to design the project, set up equipment, gather materials, produce, and clean up for that project. You can record shop cleanup time for estimating overhead, but don't include it in your project labor worksheet figures.

Labor costs are more than the hourly wage you pay yourself and/or your workers. Labor costs must also include employment taxes you pay, health or retirement benefits you pay, the cost of uniforms and related expenses. Remember, if you are the sole employee, pay yourself at least as much as you would pay an employee with your skills. I'll cover setting your shop rate in the coming pages.

Your Time and Your Skills

What is it you're selling when you sell your labor? It's more than just your time. You're also selling your creativity, your originality, your knowledge and your skills. If you produce a one-of-a-kind hand-carved work of art, your creativity, originality, knowledge and skills are extensive and you may earn thousands of dollars for your product. If you build antique clock cases, you will be paid for your creativity and your skills but not your originality,

because you are copying someone else's creative design. If you mass-produce wooden kitchen tools, your skills may be high but creativity and originality are probably not — and you will be paid accordingly for your labor.

Remember that estimating labor for your time and skills requires efficient use of both. A lawn chair that you build over a weekend doesn't require two days to build. When estimating actual working time, estimate how much time it would take to build the product if you did it all day every day. That same lawn chair may take only 2.5 hours of actual production time. By reducing production time you can increase your hourly shop rate. In fact, one of the keys to making more money as a woodworker is using your knowledge and experience to increase your productivity. The more you can do in an hour, the more you make per hour.

One way of maintaining a lower retail price to meet competition while still earning a fair shop rate is to develop production techniques that help increase quantity without reducing quality. By investing in special tools that add $4 an hour to your shop rate, you may be able to increase your "throughput" or amount of product you can make in that hour, thus reducing your price per unit.

Defining Overhead Costs

Overhead costs are all costs other than direct materials and direct labor. Overhead is the indirect cost of making your woodworking product. Overhead costs include rent (or a portion of the cost of your home), tools, electricity, telephone, taxes and miscellaneous expenses.

Figure 1-3 offers a way of estimating your overhead costs. You can either make entries directly on this worksheet or transfer them from other records you keep. Let's look at each overhead cost individually.

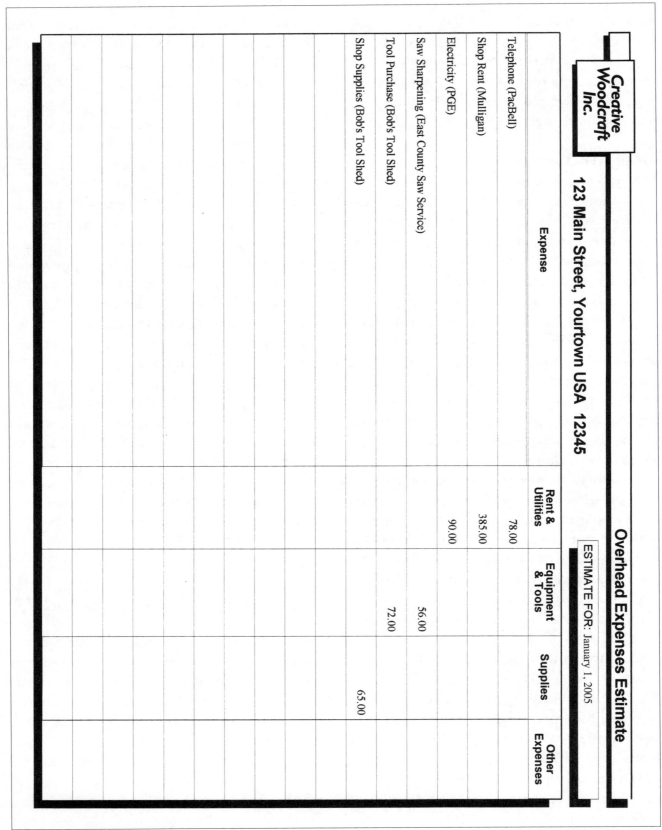

Creative Woodcraft Inc.

123 Main Street, Yourtown USA 12345

Overhead Expenses Estimate

ESTIMATE FOR: January 1, 2005

Expense	Rent & Utilities	Equipment & Tools	Supplies	Other Expenses
Telephone (PacBell)	78.00			
Shop Rent (Mulligan)	385.00			
Electricity (PGE)	90.00			
Saw Sharpening (East County Saw Service)		56.00		
Tool Purchase (Bob's Tool Shed)		72.00		
Shop Supplies (Bob's Tool Shed)			65.00	

Figure 1-3. By estimating and grouping your expenses, you can determine the fixed costs, or overhead, required to operate your woodworking venture. A blank form that you can reproduce and use is included in the appendix.

Rent

If you rent a shop for your woodworking, this is an easy calculation. You simply enter the amount of your monthly rent or lease payment. However, most hobby woodworkers start in their garage. Can you deduct some costs of your home if you use a portion of it to make money? Call the Internal Revenue Service Forms Hotline at 800-829-3676 and ask them to send you "Business Use of Your Home" (Publication 587). (Or go on the Internet to www.irs.gov; see chapter six.) It will help you determine whether you can deduct part of your home as a business and lists the expenses you can include. Other valuable tax publications are listed in chapter five.

Tools

Tools are a vital part of your woodworking; you can't work wood without them. They are a cost of production. So they are a legitimate expense as you begin selling your woodworking. A $45 caliper and a $200 biscuit joiner are both overhead expenses if you use them to make a profit with your wood-working.

As you purchase more expensive tools you can either "expense" or depreciate them for tax purposes. To expense a tool you simply include the entire cost as an expense during the year you buy the tool. Refer to IRS Publication 535 "Business Expenses". The cost of a $1,000 planer can be a deductible expense for that year even though you may use it for five years. If you depreciate the same planer over the five years, you can deduct $200 a year as an expense. Depreciation should be left up to accountants as there are many ways to depreciate tools. Once your woodworking business has grown, you can talk to an accountant about this opportunity.

Whether you expense or depreciate your tools at tax time, you need to calculate their approximate cost so you know how much to charge for overhead. If you expect to use your new $400 lathe for three years, then sell it for $100, the lathe costs you about $8.35 per month — plus the cost of maintenance and repairs.

Or you can calculate cost based on normal business loan rates on your total investment in large tools. For example, if the total investment in power tools is $1,000 and the current rate for business loans is 7 percent, your monthly capital cost is $58.83.

First step: List all your tools and their current value on this worksheet. Group tools as needed: four combination squares = $112. Include an estimate of their expected life before you will need to replace them. Depending on use, some tools will be upgraded every year while others can be replaced every ten years.

If you own or are considering buying a computer for your woodworking venture (see chapter six), it's a tool subject to the same issues as your other tools.

Utilities

Utilities are next. Estimate the cost of electricity, telephone and other utility expenses on a monthly basis. If you use your personal telephone to take business calls, you should deduct only the cost of long-distance business calls. However, if you have installed a second phone or a second line in your workshop, you can include the cost as part of your overhead expenses.

Taxes

Taxes are a part of your overhead expenses, too. You will have to pay income tax on any supplemental income from your woodworking (less expenses). In fact, if you start making serious money with your woodworking, the federal and many state governments will require you to make estimated tax payments every three months. The free IRS booklets discussed previously will get you started. For most hobby woodworkers, the amount of taxes they pay is minimal. Some simply have their full-time employer take out an extra $100 a month to cover possible tax liability from their part-time woodworking business.

Make sure you find out if craftspeople in your area are required to charge sales tax on retail sales of woodworking. If so, call your state revenue office to determine how and when to do so. While state sales taxes are not a cost of doing business for you, their collection can add to your costs. This is not a requirement if you sell all your products wholesale to retailers, but you may be responsible for an inventory tax. Check with state and local governments.

Establishing Your Profit

How much profit should you expect to make as you sell your woodworking projects? The simplest answer is that you should receive a return on your investment equal to what you would receive if you invested it somewhere else with equal risk. That is, if all your tools and your shop are worth about $5,000, what interest would you earn if you invested that money in someone else's woodworking business? The answer is typically between 10 and 20 percent. That's the return on investment you should expect from investing in your operation.

What is profit? It's the money you have left from what you sell once you've paid your expenses. It's figured like this:

Sales - Total Costs = Profit

So if you sell $20,000 worth of woodworking products that cost you $18,000 to make, your gross profit is $2,000, or 10 percent. But it's not quite that simple. Your wages as a business owner/manager and a woodworker should be considered part of the total costs. However, the tax man considers your wages to be part of your profits. For the purpose of figuring how to price your woodworking,

though, consider your wages as part of the total costs and think of profit as your reward for being crazy enough to be your own boss.

Many successful woodworkers keep track of woodworking income, expenses and profit on a computer using a spreadsheet program. Once a month they make all entries and determine whether the business is making a profit. If the profit is lower than the goal the woodworker reduces expenses as appropriate. The woodworker may hold off purchasing a secondary tool or stocking up on materials, or may reduce the owner's wages for the month to ensure that the profit goal is reached. Chapter six will cover ways of using computers and technology in your woodworking venture.

Setting Your Shop Rate

Why do you need to keep such close track of your time and expenses? Because you are going to be paid for them. Once you've developed a "shop rate" you will multiply it by the time it takes to perform the task to determine the labor costs. As an example, you will multiply a shop rate of $35 times the 1.2 hours it took to build the 12" × 16" drawer to come up with a labor cost of $42.

SHOP RATE	TIME	JOB	LABOR COST
$40.00	1.2 hrs.	12" × 16" drawer	$48.00

Now the big question: What should your shop rate be? Most professional woodworking shops charge $35 to $70 an hour. That's their shop rate. It typically includes the worker's wage, overhead and sometimes even profit. If you post your shop rate, telling others what your hourly rate is (not recommended), make sure that a profit margin is included in it. If you use your shop rate only in calculating estimates, you can have a profit margin

Creative Woodcraft Inc.

JOB EXPENSE RECORD

DATE June 1, 2005

JOB DESCRIPTION

Build and finish living room table set: coffee and two tables per drawing 40012

	DATE	ITEM	Net Cost	Markup	Total Cost
MATERIALS		Coffee table	96.11	96.11	192.22
		Corner table	74.55	74.55	149.10
		End table	57.22	57.22	114.44
		Total	$227.88	$227.88	$455.76

	DATE	Name	Hours	Rate	Net Cost	Markup	Total Cost
LABOR		Bob	6	35.00	210.00	63.00	273.00
		Mary	2	35.00	70.00	21.00	91.00
				Total	$280.00	$84.00	$364.00

	DATE	DESCRIPTION	AMOUNT
MISCELLANEOUS EXPENSES			
		Total	

	Net Cost	Markup	Total Cost
Total Materials	227.88	$227.88	$455.76
Total Labor	$280.00	$84.00	$364.00
Total Miscellaneous			
Grand Total	$507.88	$311.88	$819.76

Figure 1-4. Use a Job Expense Record to record the cost of materials, labor and other expenses to determine the cost of a woodworking job. A blank form that you can reproduce and use is included in the appendix.

that is added into your estimate once materials, labor and overhead are figured in.

As an example, a skilled woodworker feels that he would have to pay $18 an hour to hire himself. He then adds the cost of a benefits package (⅓, or $6 per hour). Overhead comes to $7.50 per hour to cover rent, tools, utilities and basic supplies. He wants a profit of 10 percent on the total. He rounds off the total to $35 and sets that amount as his "posted" shop rate.

Basic labor rate (per hour)	$18.00
Benefits (⅓ of labor rate)	$6.00
Overhead	$7.50
Subtotal	$31.50
Profit — 10% of subtotal	$3.15
Total	$34.65
Shop Rate	$35.00

Remember that your shop rate is your number for calculating costs and setting pricing. In most cases, you won't tell your customers what your shop rate is. They don't know what it involves and cannot compare your shop rate to anyone else's but their own — which you usually don't want them to do.

Think your shop rate is high? Ask your attorney, accountant or other professional what their hourly rate is and you'll find that the shop rate for woodworkers is quite a value. Figure 1-4 shows how it all comes together.

Developing a Price Sheet

By keeping good records, you determine that you can build and finish six identical mechanical whirligigs in about 3 hours, that materials cost you around $24, and that overhead (tools, utilities, taxes, etc.) and profit are built into your shop rate of $35 an hour. So you estimate that six whirligigs can profitably be built for $129 (3 hours @ $35/hour + $24 for materials). That's $21.50 per whirligig. You might then price them at $21.50

each, or $24.95 each with the second one at $17.95, or you may decide to price red ones at $24.95 and multicolor ones at $17.95. Or you can look at what competitors get for their whirligigs and price them all at $23.95 each.

Eventually you will develop a component price sheet that is both profitable and competitive. It will list the woodworking components that you sell and the price at which you must sell them. You may or may not decide to give copies to potential customers, depending on how easy the price sheet is to use. Remember, too, that if you give out a price sheet, you must make sure that you give new ones to the same people as you change your pricing. Component pricing allows you to estimate a project faster than figuring every task. Component pricing for a kitchen-cabinet maker will list the price for each finished cabinet by size, the price of countertops by running or square feet, and the typical installation charge for each.

Here's a tip from many successful woodworkers I interviewed: Pricing your products to beat the competition is a good idea, but make sure it's a price that also covers your costs. If it doesn't, find a product that has less competition and a better opportunity for you to earn a profit at what you enjoy doing.

Maybe you have already established a shop rate that is lower than the $35 to $70 an hour of most professional woodshops. How can you increase your shop rate to this level? First, make sure you are working as efficiently as possible. Chapter five will include a number of proven ideas on how to make your shop more efficient. Chapter six offers tips on using technology to increase profits. The key to a higher shop rate is higher efficiency. Second, once you've established your new shop rate, set a date when it will become effective and let your prospects and customers know. It will give you more business now — as prospects order before the price increase — and will give you more profit later as your shop rate goes up.

A Pricing Method

One popular method of pricing a product or service — one that can easily be applied to pricing your woodworking — is called YECH (rhymes with "etch") Pricing. YECH is an acronym that stands for:

YOU

ECONOMY

COMPETITION and

HUNGER

Your Costs

Here's how it works. First, add up all the direct and indirect costs required to make and sell your woodworking product. You estimate direct materials costs, set your labor costs, define indirect or overhead costs and establish your profit margin, just as illustrated above.

The Economy

Second, you consider the economy in the area where your woodworking products will sell. Is the economy growing and do customers have money for discretionary spending? Or is unemployment high and do people have little money for fine woodcrafts? If your economy is not strong, consider selling your woodworking products in a region that is, or in a nearby community where people with higher incomes live and purchase (see chapter five). What are the economic conditions of the prospective customers? Are they conditioned to expect high price tags that allow you to invest more time in your products? Or are they looking for something that will do the job at the lowest cost?

The Competition

Third, always look at what your competition is selling and the price they are getting. Remember that your competition is not just someone selling an item exactly like yours; it is anyone who competes for the same dollar. That is, if you make coffee-table decorations, other woodworkers who make crafts to decorate a living room are your competitors. They're going after the same dollar that you are. How are they doing? What are they selling? For how much? In your experienced opinion, what are their direct and indirect costs? How can you compete with them and still make a fair profit?

Hunger

Finally, pricing is controlled by hunger. Your hunger. All your calculations of indirect costs (overhead) are based on a specific amount of sales. If your overhead costs are $250 a month and you expect to make 10 units in a month, the indirect costs are $25 per unit — if you sell 10. But if you sell just one unit that month, the indirect costs for that single unit are the full $250. So you may decide to sell a few units more at a discount in order to recoup part of your overhead. Or you may be hungry to make a sale to a specific client and decide to discount a piece to do so.

Here's the other side of hunger: You're full. You have enough work to keep you busy for the foreseeable future, but one customer insists that he must have one of your woodworking projects by the end of next week. So you price the project at a premium. You pay yourself overtime. Later in this book, I'll tell you more about what to do when you're too busy.

Problem Projects

One more point: You'll have some projects or some people that you know will become a problem. The project will require additional time to search for matching stock, or the customer is a grumbler who will not be satisfied until he's returned it to you three times. Many professional workers add what they call a PITA fee to these types of projects. PITA is an acronym for "pain in the anterior". The trick is determining which projects should include this "fee" in the pricing. Other woodworkers figure that about 10 percent of their projects will include difficult tasks or people and add this into their shop rate. Experience will guide you.

What if the custom project you quoted changes during its development but after you've given a price? Should you increase or reduce the price? For example, you're building custom outdoor furniture for a customer to whom you've already quoted a price of $800. The customer wants better grade wood than you specified in the price. Who pays?

The hard-and-fast rule is: It depends. If the customer changes the requirements, he or she should pay. If you change the requirements, you should pay. If you or the customer downgrades the specs, the customer should get the cost reduction. In the above example, the customer should pay for the cost of the upgrade as well as any additional labor and costs you incur by the change (more sanding and finishing time, etc.). If, rather, you and the customer agree that the grade of wood can be downgraded without any reduction in features, the customer gets the difference.

The problem is making sure that everyone understands the changes and how they affect the price in advance of making the changes. For custom work, your estimate should include a place to write any changes made to the project and the cost of those changes, and a place for you and the customer to sign or initial. Don't depend on memory or on verbal agreements. If it is important, get it in writing. If it isn't important, give the change to the customer free of charge.

Price vs. Volume

In establishing your pricing, you have estimated the volume or amount of sales you expect to make. The price-vs.-volume issue has two sides. Should you go for higher prices and lower volume, or

should you try to sell more with a lower price? No single correct answer fits everyone. Much depends on YECH:

YOU: Do you prefer to sell a few or many?
ECONOMY: Does your market prefer lower price or higher quality?
COMPETITION: Does your competition sell price or quality?
HUNGER: Which will best help you pay your expenses?

For example, a cabinetmaker preferred to produce high-quality cabinets for luxury homes in his area, but the economy changed and such homes weren't being built. He did learn that many homeowners were upgrading their bathrooms and that this local market was not adequately served. So, temporarily, he began building bathroom vanities and mirrored cabinets for homeowners and remodelers. In fact, he used the reputation he had built as a high-price cabinetmaker to help sell his more reasonably priced cabinets. His answer to the price-vs.-volume question is: Follow the needs of the market.

How to Sell Value Over Price

Thus far, the emphasis has been to learn exactly what your cost of producing a woodworking product is before you set the price. This method ensures that you will cover your actual expenses and make a reasonable return on your investment and skills. However, your best opportunities for profitability are to sell on value rather than on price.

Frankly, people who buy woodcrafts don't want something that looks like it came from a discount store. More and more consumers want products that have their own personality — and are willing to pay for it. They want value!

What a decorative wooden box cost you to make is really irrelevant to the buyer. The real issue is: What is the box worth to the buyer? How much money will buyers give you in exchange for the benefits that this wooden box gives them? The answer is: That depends on how many of the benefits the buyers can see and value. Your job as an artisan is to help buyers see the value of your woodworking product.

The buyer can go to a stationery store and buy a small box to place things in. That's utility value. In this case, utility value may be $6. Or the buyer can find a decorative wooden box mass-produced with minimal artistic value for $20. That's craft value. Or the buyer can purchase your handmade wooden box made from native woods, hand-sanded and skillfully finished to ensure a smooth and precise fit, for $60. That's artistic value. Why should the buyer purchase your box at 10 times the cost of the utility box? Because she understands and values the difference between the two.

Selling the Artistic Value

To sell the artistic value of your woodworking product you must first understand its utility value and its craft value, because you are competing with both. As an example, if you make high-quality kitchen cabinets, you should know the price a customer will have to pay for basic utility kitchen cabinets that serve the same function. You should also know how much a customer will pay for factory-built cabinets of moderate quality. These cabinets are your competition. By knowing these prices you can help your customers understand the value they will receive by paying more for your quality cabinets.

Copyrighting Your Work

One proven way to sell value over price is to copyright your work. Besides the obvious protection a copyright gives you as a creative woodworker, it also tells your customers that your products are unique. A copyright gives the creator/designer the exclusive right to control how, where and when the design is used. This includes reproducing, selling, distributing or displaying the work. These rights belong to the creator during his or her lifetime plus 70 years for individual works and 75 to 95 years for corporate works and works first published before January 1, 1998.

An idea cannot be copyrighted, but the execution of an idea can be. So a wooden chest cannot be copyrighted, but its unique shape or design can be. That's called "artistic craftsmanship."

You can copyright your work by simply putting a copyright notice on the work:

Copyright 2005, Waldo Woodworker

If you plan to sue anyone who infringes on your design copyright, you will also want to register the copyright. To do so, write to the Library of Congress, U.S. Copyright Office, 101 Independence Avenue, S.E., Washington, DC 20559, for the required forms and current fee. Ask for Form VA (for registering "visual arts"). The current copyright registration fee is $30. The Library of Congress's copyright service is on the Internet at www.copyright.gov.

Why Customers Ask the Price

Most woodworkers who shop for new equipment attempt to balance two factors: price and value. Few people buy on price alone. Before selecting a band saw, for example, the typical woodworker considers the features and translates them into benefits. A tilting table on the band saw is a feature. Having a table that tilts up to 45°, allowing the woodworker to cut pieces needed in making popular wooden toys, for example, is a benefit. If the benefit makes the woodworker's job easier, faster or more profitable, it is a useful benefit that has value.

Specific brands of tools or materials may also have a valued benefit. You may select one brand of band saw over another because your experience — and advertising messages — tell you that owning that brand gives you prestige, quality or peace of mind.

As a customer for a new tool, you will ask the price to decide whether the two factors — price and value — are equal. In offering the price, the catalog copy or the salesperson will tell you about the features and benefits of this tool so you can determine value for yourself. Or the salesperson may ask you about your specific needs, then help you define the tool's value in terms of those needs. But you must make the final decision because you are the customer.

Illustrating Value

How about your customers? How can you illustrate the value of your woodworking product to them? The answer depends on the features and benefits that your product offers to customers. If you make and sell salad bowl sets, you can display them on a small decorative table with a fine tablecloth, utensils and maybe a vase of flowers. You can cut a bowl in half to show that it is made of solid wood. You can display the set next to a list of its features and benefits:

- Quality craftsmanship (feature) for long, useful life (benefit).
- Hand-selected woods (feature) add beauty to your table (benefit).
- Durable finish (feature) stands up to daily use (benefit).

You get the picture. In order to sell the value of your woodworking product, you must make sure customers understand the product's features and benefits in their own terms.

Figure 1-5 illustrates a list of features and benefits for a woodworking product. You can develop your own list for the products you make and sell. A blank copy of the form is included in the appendix of this book for your use. Write your own name at the head of the form (or paste your business card) and take it to a copy shop.

Selling the Value of Your Work

Customers will always want to know the price of your work. That's their nature. You, as a craftsperson, want to make sure they understand the value of your work as well so they can make an informed decision about purchasing it. Depending on what you make and how you sell it, many ways exist to help you ensure that your customers know the value of your products as they make that decision.

One successful woodcarver knows that most customers who pick up a piece at his craft booth turn it over to look for a price sticker on the bottom. So he placed stickers on all his pieces that said, "Great value! Ask me the price." After reading the sticker, most customers would look up to see the craftsman. Knowing this, he would watch anyone who picked up one of his carvings and try to be ready with eye contact and a smile when they looked up. He would then "break the ice" with a comment like, "That's a one-of-a-kind carving." In most cases, the customer would then ask the price and the craftsman would respond with more comments about its value: "I hand-selected that wood because of the unique graining in it. I can sign the base if you'd like." The craftsman wanted his customer to set a dollar value in their mind before telling them the price. He found that, in most

Creative Woodcraft Inc.

Features & Benefits Worksheet

123 Main Street, Yourtown USA 12345

Product: Rocking Chair

FEATURE What does it have?	BENEFIT Why is it important?
* Solid oak, no laminates	* Will last many years and become an heirloom
* Constructed with dowels, not screws	* No fasteners to work loose
* Hand-caned seat and back	* Quality caning offers custom fit for long life
* Six coats of finish	* Finish will stand up to frequent use while
	keeping its beauty and protection
* Many hours to construct	* Built with quality craftsmanship to be enjoyed
	for many years
* Sold directly to customers	* No marketing costs means the savings are
	passed on to the customer

Figure 1-5. A Features & Benefits Worksheet helps you see your product in terms of the customer's needs. A blank form that you can reproduce and use is included in the appendix.

cases, the customers would value the piece at or above his actual price. The craftsman didn't make a sale every time, but his sales increased because he sold value before he told price.

Should You Use Price Tags?

Should you place a price tag on your items or not? Much depends on what you sell, to whom and when. Woodworking products under about $100 are typically priced; items above that amount may be if the prospective buyers are price-shoppers. If they are upscale buyers (such as in a gallery), pricing does not need to appear on the item.

If you change the price, should you write over the old price on the sticker? In most cases, no, especially if you have increased the price. Unless your woodcraft is facing tough pricing competition, you should remove the old sticker and put a new sticker on the item with the new price. You should also periodically replace any price stickers that look worn or faded; you don't want customers to think you haven't been able to sell the product since the Ice Age. Never apologize to your customers for your pricing; instead, describe the value.

Odd Pricing

Let's talk about "odd pricing" before moving on. Odd pricing is the setting of a price that is just under a whole dollar amount. Instead of $30, an odd-priced item is $29.99, $29.95, $29.89, etc. Odd pricing was begun many years ago to give the illusion of a lower or bargain price. It is so widely used in pricing everything from crackers to cars that many people round it off in their heads: "about thirty bucks."

Should a woodworker use odd pricing? Much depends on what you're selling and for how much. If you sell inexpensive woodworking products that the consumer can purchase from other sources, consider using odd pricing, especially for items under $10. However, for most woodworking products, prices should be rounded off to the nearest 50

cents for items under $10, the nearest $1 between $11 and $50, the nearest $5 between $51 and $100, the nearest $10 between $100 and $250, and the nearest $50 above $250. For example, if you decide that the retail price should be about $114, round it up to $120.

Salesmanship

Some people think that "selling" is a dirty word. A craftsperson doesn't actually "sell" his or her woodworking product. The craftsperson helps potential customers learn why they will benefit from buying the product. Simply talking with people about what you do, why, and how it will benefit them is the best form of salesmanship. Selling, too, is a craft. The more that you talk to people honestly about their needs and your solutions, the more you will sell. No magic formulas or passwords are necessary. Knowledge and sincerity are still the best sales tools. Of course, don't talk politics, religion, or anything controversial with customers.

Finally, never wait for the customer to say, "I'll take it." Whenever the customer shows an interest in your woodworking by asking a specific question or by commenting on your work, "close" the sale with a comment or question that helps the customer commit to her internal decision. "Thank you. Can I gift wrap it for you?" Or "Yes, it's hand-sanded and finished. Would you like to have one?" Or "I'm very proud of that piece. Would you prefer the golden oak or the red oak?"

Selling to Friends, Relatives and Neighbors

Chances are, your first customers will be friends, relatives and neighbors. Why? Because the best advertising is word-of-mouth. Someone gets your woodworking as a gift, shows it to someone else who tells a third party whose son-in-law buys one. This is a great way to start making money with your woodworking.

But it can also be a problem. How much do you charge your best friend for those decorative turnings that you make? What if your neighbor asks you to build and install a bath vanity like the one in your home? What if a friend of a friend wants a discount on your Shaker furniture?

Stick to Your Pricing

The best way to avoid problems and hurt feelings is to have a pricing policy and stick to it. That is, you decide in advance how much of your woodworking you give away as gifts, how much you will discount any of your works and under what conditions.

As an example, one successful woodworker decided that he could not afford to give any of his antique reproductions as gifts. Instead, he made a specific number of small wooden puzzles during his slow season each year and gave them out as gifts through the coming year. When they were gone, they were gone. He did, however, offer discounts to friends and acquaintances — if they promised to tell others about his work but not to tell anyone the amount of the discount they were given. He then offered a 20 percent discount to friends and relatives and a 10 percent discount to acquaintances. He considered this a sales commission: these people would become his sales staff and tell others about his work. He didn't give away his work. Nor did he give away the discount. He traded the discount for something of value: word-of-mouth advertising.

No Freebies

What do you say to friends and relatives who ask for free products? You're going to tell them no, but you need to do it in a way that will strengthen your relationship. You can say, "I'm really glad you like my work. I've spent many years developing my skills and many dollars on my equipment. And I use only the best materials I can find. I'm sure you understand that I can't just give them away. But I value our relationship. Let me do this: I'll give you a full 20 percent (or 10 percent) discount on anything I make if you'll tell others about my work. Of course, you can't tell anyone I've given you a special deal. That takes all my profit, but I'm willing to do it for you."

If the friend, relative or neighbor still insists on a better price, talk to them about value. Tell them why your woodworking product is valuable to them. Mention the features and how those features will benefit them. Sell them on value. If that still doesn't work, you can either give your time, skills and materials away, or you can say, "I'm sorry, but no."

Selling "Art"

You can add value to your woodworking products — and command a higher price — by making each of your products unique. A craft product is typically a copy of a unique design. Other copies are out there and the customer knows it. A piece of art is unique in itself.

You may be making wooden toy cars from a specific design, each car nearly identical to all the others. If you set them all out on a table, a customer would think they are all the same — and pay you accordingly. But if you add something artful to each one, they are now unique and are worth more to the customer and to you.

Adding Art to Craft

How can you make each of your woodworking products unique without pricing yourself out of the market with extra labor costs? If you make wooden toy cars, produce some components by hand rather than by machine. Hand-carve a hood ornament, paint each car uniquely, modify some of them to be coupes or convertibles, offer to etch the owner's name on the radiator or even number each of your cars on the undercarriage.

The more unique you make your woodworking products, the more they become art rather than craft. Wooden picture frames can be made unique by hand-carving part of the trim design. Birdhouses can be made more artistic by adding freehand gingerbread to the roof. Candlesticks can be made more artistic by adding unique hand-painted designs to each pair. Wooden boxes can have your name burned into the base. Even selecting exotic woods with varying patterns can give the product a unique and artistic quality.

By adding artistic elements to your craft you also develop your artistic skills. Then, as your skills grow, you can command an even higher price as you produce truly one-of-a-kind pieces for discriminating customers.

Give a Little Extra

Here's another proven idea: Rather than facing competitors in a pricing war, offer extra services. That is, offer to gift wrap, or to accept out-of-area checks or payment by charge card. Art is not simply your product, but also your service and how you present yourself.

How to Show Your Woodworking

Successful woodworkers know not only how to price their work, but also how to show it so customers can see its value. Depending on what you make, your area of the country and how you feel about salesmanship, you have many options for showing your products.

Smaller items, such as toy cars, boxes, desk accessories, candlesticks, jewelry and carvings, can be easily shown with a sample. When prospective customers ask about your product you have a sample you can hand them to examine as you point out its features and benefits.

Use Photos for Larger Items

Larger items are more difficult to move and display. This is especially true of woodworking products that must be installed to be functional, such as kitchen or bathroom cabinetry. In this case, the best sales tool is photos of completed projects. If you're handy with a camera, you can take these photos yourself. Otherwise you may want to have a professional or at least more experienced photographer take your photos.

Place your photos in a quality three-ring binder or presentation binder. A presentation binder, available at larger stationery stores, allows you to stand the binder up on its edge for display. Include sample literature, business cards, and letters from happy customers. Of course, also include any awards, competitions, commissions, reviews and professional credentials that underscore your acceptance as an artist. You'll have a presentation kit that will help you sell your woodworking at a fair price.

Even if you show your projects with photos, make sure you have something that the customer can touch and hold, such as a cabinet door, a chest top or even a miniature of the final product. Also, give your prospective customers something to select from, but don't overload them with 39 flavors.

And once you have your own Internet Web site (see chapter six), you can share photos of your products with the world. I'll tell you more about taking and using digital photos as well. You can save digital photos to CDs and share them with potential customers.

Venues for Showing Your Work

Where will you show your wares? Typically not in your shop. You may want to impress your customers with a photo of your cleaned-up shop to illustrate the many tools you need to make their purchase — or you may decide that having a picture isn't worth the trouble of cleaning up your shop! In either case, most customers are sold at their own home or place of business (depending on where they will use it) or in a buying/selling environment such as a craft show. People will buy what they can see or visualize. If your product is too large to transport or is a custom piece that must be designed to fit specific needs, your best visualization method is a photo of a similar finished product.

One enterprising custom furniture maker using his garage as a shop put up a false wall six feet from the main door and used the space as his showroom. He sealed the room from shop dust, laid a carpet remnant down, paneled the area and set up samples of his work as well as finished items awaiting pickup or delivery.

Catalogs, Brochures and Business Cards

Depending on your woodworking product, you can show it or pictures of it in person, in a catalog or in a brochure. Even if you have a sample to show people, you may want a brochure that describes your services, your products and your attitude toward your work. Many print shops have the capability to turn your ideas and photos into a simple brochure. The finished brochure can then be given to people at craft shows, to friends and relatives, to other artisans, mailed to prospective customers or to sales representatives, or passed out at the shopping mall. They make an inexpensive and practical way of telling others about your woodworking and how they will benefit from calling you.

One successful woodworker sold his frames at craft fairs. He held a drawing at each event for an impressive, but inexpensive, frame. Those who signed up for the drawing were sent a brochure, price sheet and order form for his other frames during the next week.

Many ways are available to inexpensively promote your woodworking venture. A brochure is one of the best. Another is through business cards. A local printer, copy shop or desktop publishing shop can help you design and write effective business cards. They can be given to friends, relatives and acquaintances, tacked up on local bulletin boards or traded with noncompeting craftspeople. If you have a particularly photogenic product, you can have its picture taken and used as the background of your business card.

Other successful woodworking businesses have postcards printed with pictures of their products on the back side and information about their business on the left half of the front. These cards can serve as business cards, brochures and mailing pieces. Be creative in your marketing as well as in your craft.

Again, the Internet offers many profitable ways of showing and selling your woodworking. Chapter six will introduce you to using technology for profit.

Developing a Reputation for Quality

Quality is the primary characteristic of excellence; it is the best it can be under the circumstances. A quality cabinet is made of the best woods available for the money spent, is built with knowledgeable craftsmanship and careful consideration is given to detail. Quality is not perfection. It is what it should be: functional and aesthetic.

Most woodworkers strive for quality. They want to apply their skills and their self to making functional and beautiful things from wood. They understand that building a reputation for quality can somewhat limit the business that they do, but it is worth the effort.

Set Your Own Standard

Being a quality woodworker doesn't necessarily mean that others will see the quality that is put into each job. What should you do? Should you lower your standard? Should you maintain quality and price yourself out of the market? These are tough questions that every professional woodworker must answer.

Some woodworkers decide that spending additional hours in details that the customers will neither see nor appreciate is part of their standard of quality. Other woodworkers feel that it is not true quality if it does not directly benefit the customer. In fact, they contend that unrecognized quality prices an otherwise valuable product out of the hands of all but a few buyers. They would rather reach more buyers with good quality than only a few buyers with perfection. Some woodworkers disagree and feel that quality requires coming as close to perfection as possible.

Which viewpoint is correct? The answer is: all and none. Quality is not an absolute but a standard. You establish your own standard for the work you do, and in order to sell your woodworking, that standard must meet the standard established by the buyer. If it exceeds the buyer's standard, it will also probably exceed his or her ability to pay.

Build Your Reputation

Once you've decided what standard of quality works best for you and your prospective customers, you can decide how best to build your reputation for quality. You may want to develop a reputation for using only the most exotic woods, for bringing the best out of common woods or for using hardwoods in new ways (you certainly don't want to develop a reputation for doing all things with all woods). Or your standard of quality may be defined as building wooden toys that will be handed down from father to son for many generations.

How do you promote your standard of quality? Obviously you do so by the work you do. But you can also build your reputation for quality by simply defining your attitude toward your work and making sure that others know what it is. You can choose a slogan that clearly reflects your attitudes toward quality:

- Bringing out the hidden beauty of pine through decorative boxes.
- Building oak cabinetry that reflects your good taste.
- Making functional lawn furniture that lasts a lifetime.
- Fabricating antique reproductions at a fraction of the cost of originals.
- Offering the fastest whirligigs in the world.

Your attitude toward workmanship becomes the slogan for your woodworking business. It tells others what you do and why you do it. Use this slogan on your business cards, literature and Web site. Have it reproduced on small labels with your name and address, and attach the labels to every piece you make. It will help you develop your reputation for quality. It will also help you sell your woodworking at a fair price.

Using a Business Name

One proven method of developing a reputation for quality is giving your woodworking venture a quality name. For example, an enterprising woodworker in Sacramento, California, named her business High Sierra Outdoor Furniture. It gave customers an image of a large firm that was in touch with nature. They didn't know that her shop was one-half of a double garage and that she and her son are the entire workforce. The image worked and her business eventually outgrew the garage because she named her business for the size she wanted it to be rather than what it was.

A fictitious business name is a name other than the real and true name of each person operating a business. A real and true name becomes a fictitious business name with the addition of any words that are not your own name. For example, "Bob Smith" is a real and true name, while "Bob Smith Company" is a fictitious business name.

In most states and counties, you must register a fictitious business name to let the public know who is transacting business under that name. Without the registration you may be fined; worse, you may not be able to defend a legal action because your assumed business name wasn't properly registered.

In many states, a fictitious business name is registered with the state's corporate division. Some states will also register your fictitious business name with counties in which you do business. Other states require that you do so. In some locations, you must publish a public notice in an area newspaper stating that you (and any other business principals) are operating under a specific business name.

In most communities, you may also need a local business license. The best way to learn what the requirements are for your area is to contact your state government. Some states have a "one-stop" business telephone number where you can find out what the requirements are, or at least the phone numbers of governing offices.

How to Negotiate for Fun and Profit

Woodworker Nancy Bartow of Scholfield Valley Wood Products retails her hand mirrors and earring holders at craft shows. She says that 95 percent of her customers are pleasant, and most don't try to negotiate price. About 5 percent use rudeness as a negotiation tool. If the price is $100, they want it for $50; if the same item was $50, they would demand it for $25. We all know of people like this. But in selling your woodworking, how do you keep from giving away your time and talents to these people for free?

The first step is to know what you must get for your product. You've learned what this price is by determining the time it takes to make your product, setting a value for your time, knowing the cost of materials and establishing the amount of profit you need to make. You know, for example, that you must get at least $75 for your wooden dollhouse in order to cover materials and labor costs and to make a minimum return on your investment.

Giving the Customer a Good Deal

From this point, you can price your products to take into account the fact that some people will not buy from you unless they can get a "deal." To them, it's not the amount but the fact that they got it for less than other people pay. It's a matter of pride with them. If you sell at craft shows, a higher percentage of people will want to deal than if you sell wholesale to gift shops. You price accordingly. You sell the dollhouse to gift shops at $125 each, and you price them at craft shows at $175 each to cover show costs and allow for negotiation.

Remember that the *H* in YECH pricing stands for hunger. If the show is ready to close and you don't want to take your products home with you, you may decide to offer a discount to any amount above your wholesale price.

Actually, negotiating can be fun. In fact, some woodworkers love this part of their job enough to look forward to craft shows when they can "deal" with customers face-to-face. Once you know your minimum price, you can make it a game. As long as you get your minimum price, you win and the customer wins. How much you win depends on your skills as a negotiator.

Negotiation Techniques

Here are some tips and techniques that negotiators use to make deals that are win-win situations.

What you give away has no value. If you automatically give a 10 percent discount to anyone who blinks their eyes twice, the customer feels you've inflated your price. Instead, offer to trade value for value: "I'll give you a 10 percent discount on this lawn furniture if you will write me a letter of recommendation that I can show to prospective customers." Of course, you really don't have to enforce your must-have-a-letter rule unless you want to, but making it a bargaining tool does give your discount greater value.

Offer an alternative piece. If a customer wants to offer you $125 for your $150 riding toy, offer one that is unfinished or a demonstration model that has seen use. Or you can offer less-than-perfect items that are kept under the counter. Label them "Woodworking I Did before My First Cup of Coffee."

Ask, "If I sell it to you for that price, what will you do for me?" Some people will offer to send friends to you or give you something of value. Others won't. What you decide to accept in trade is up to you. The point is that you show that the discount you give them has real value.

Trading Discounts

Ask your customers what they do for a living, then ask for an equal discount from them. If the customer owns a restaurant, ask for an equal amount of free meals. If they work in a gas station, are they authorized to trade fuel with you? Again, whether the deal is accepted or not, the customers realize that the discount they requested has monetary value. You can then suggest a smaller discount or a token trade, or simply give the discount because you want them as customers. In each case, the customers understand that they have received something of value and not just a valueless discount.

Bidding Wars

Another technique: Respond to a low bid by restating it and asking for a higher bid: "Forty-five dollars? Can't you give me a better offer than that?" It doesn't refuse the bid, it just asks for a higher one. Or you can ask in a more friendly way: "Help me. I want to sell you this, but I have to cover my costs.

Please make me a better offer."

Some woodworkers will respond to a low bid with points of value until the customer offers what they consider is an acceptable price.

CUSTOMER: I'll give you $180.

WOODWORKER: This clock is made with solid oak; no laminates.

CUSTOMER: I'll make it $190.

WOODWORKER: The works are imported from Germany. You have to wind it only once a week, and it will keep excellent time.

CUSTOMER: $200.

WOODWORKER: Sold!

Sometimes the best response to a ludicrous offer is to ignore it. Another is to use humor. Say with a smile, "I'll give you $2 for that shirt you're wearing!" Humor can defuse the situation and give you a chance to think of a more appropriate response to their request for a discount, such as, "Why?"

Maintaining Your Pricing

"My brother Harry bought one of these from you last year for fifty bucks less. I want the same deal!"

How can you maintain your pricing when many people ask for special deals and friend-of-a-friend discounts? The same rule applies: Set your price fairly and stay with it as much as you possibly can. Keep in mind that if you give too many discounts, you'll either lose money or you'll have to raise your prices to everyone to cover your costs. If you do discount, have a good reason: Competitors are selling it for less and you don't want to lose business to them; you haven't sold enough this month to cover all your overhead costs; or selling a few more will help you get a better discount from your suppliers.

THE CRAFT OF PRICING

You can also disarm discount customers by taking their side. "You're right, sir, I did sell one to your brother Harry last year for less than my current price. I certainly don't blame you for wanting one at the same price. I'll be happy to give you the same price on the same product, but I've added a number of features to it since then and use better woods. It's now worth about $100 more than last year's version, but I'm charging only $50 more." Then go on to explain the additional value.

Never confront someone who challenges your pricing. The customer isn't always right, but he is still the customer. You know what it cost to make and what you need for it. Smile and agree. Then explain the value rather than the price. Remember that some buyers will push you just to see if you really have priced your works fairly and understand their value.

The first rule of pricing has been stated many ways in this chapter to ensure that you apply it to your woodworking: Sell value over price. Make it a habit of answering any question about pricing with information about value. Only when your customer understands the value of your woodworking product should you tell him the price.

How to Reflect Cost Increases

What should you do if your supplier increases the cost of your materials? That depends. A 5 percent increase by a supplier that furnishes 20 percent of your materials equates to a 1 percent ($.05 \times .20$) increase in your material costs. By making an allowance in your pricing for such variables, you won't have to increase prices every time a supplier makes an increase. However, if your primary supplier increases prices by 100 percent, it's time to look for a new supplier or, if it is an industry-wide hike, reluctantly pass the increase on to your customers.

How to Price Seconds

Of course, woodworkers don't make mistakes. However, they do produce learning experiences and less-than-perfect products. Can you sell these second-quality products? If so, for how much?

Whether you sell your seconds and to whom depends on who your primary customer is. If your customer is a gallery and your products must represent your best work, don't try to sell them anything less. However, if you sell your woodworking products directly to the public at craft shows, you can have an area — above or beneath your display table — set aside for seconds. Identify these less-than-perfect products in some way so that your customers and those who see your products know that this is not your best work. Craftspeople who place their name or a logo on all of their work do not do so on seconds. Others write "imperfect" in an inconspicuous place such as the base or back.

So how much should you charge for seconds? Most woodworkers simply double the price of materials as long as it doesn't exceed about half of the retail price. For example, a second-quality decorative turning made from an $8 blank should be priced at about $16, unless the retail price for first-quality items is less than $32. If first-quality retails for $28, price the second at $14. Of course, the pricing of seconds also depends on how much less than perfect the product is. You may decide to donate it instead, or put it up on your I-learned-from-this shelf.

Other Techniques with Seconds

Here are two more ideas to consider when pricing less-than-perfect merchandise: First, mark the product with the full retail price, then show the discounted price. For example, the above decorative turning would be marked "Regular Price: $30; Imperfect Price: $15." Second, make sure the customer knows that all sales of imperfect products are final. You want the customer to perceive these seconds as of less value than your first-quality products; otherwise the customer will feel your regular products are overpriced.

To close a sale on a second, show the buyer how he or she can make the repair or hide the imperfection. Don't offer to do it for them, no matter how minor.

Some woodworkers will use their seconds as a lure to bring customers into the booth. Others will display seconds in a separate area. Still other craftspeople will keep seconds below the display table, bringing them out only when it looks like a sale will be lost because of price. Your technique for pricing and selling seconds depends on what you sell, how you sell and to whom. As you get the opportunity, try each of these techniques to determine which will increase your total sales and profit.

When to Raise Prices: The 80/20 Rule

You may now be thinking: $40 an hour is a lot of money; I'll never be able to get that for my work. In fact, a day will soon come when you should consider raising your shop rate. When? When your customers tell you to!

How will your customers tell you to raise prices on your woodworking? By keeping you too busy. As an example, if you find that 10 hours a week is all you want to spend carving decoys, yet you have more than enough business to fill more hours, it's time to raise your prices. Or if you've set aside your Saturdays for profitable woodworking and you're booked up for the next three months, consider increasing your shop rate or your time on each project. You have too much business.

Rather than raise prices, some woodworkers will decide to spend more time at their part-time business. They may even decide to turn it into a full-time venture within a year. But most woodworkers prefer to make more money for the hours they do work so they can have additional funds for retirement, vacations or special needs.

When Everyone's Buying ...

A good indicator that it's time to raise prices is when all those to whom you quote a price actually buy from you. The ideal is to follow the 80/20 rule: 80 percent of your prospective customers should be happy with your prices. At least 20 percent of those you give prices to should turn you down because of price. Most will be because your price is too high. Some, though, will be because your price is too low for the quality they expect.

If only 40 percent of your prospective customers are buying from you, you should consider lowering your price until you are as busy as you want to be. Once the number of buying customers increases to 80 percent or more, think about increasing your prices.

How Much to Increase

How much of a price increase should you make? Of course, that depends somewhat on what your current price is. If your shop rate is now just $25 an hour, you need to get it up to the $35 to $70 an hour that most woodworking shops get. Depending on how busy you are, you may decide to increase rates to $30 an hour now and to $35 an hour in six months if business hasn't dropped off below your desired level. Many woodworkers increase their shop rate by approximately 5 percent each year just before their busy season. Others do so every 18 months or two years.

Increase Price, Maintain Shop Rate

Another option is to increase the unit price for your woodworking product while maintaining your hourly shop rate. That is, your $150 hand-carved figures are increased in price by 10 percent to $165 each. This increase allows you to spend more time on each piece, enhancing the quality of the workmanship and, thus, increasing its value. Then, as increased value builds more sales, you can raise your prices again to reflect the enhanced value.

Because price increases are intended to drive a small amount of business away, you can offset the losses by announcing your price increase in advance. For example, if your china hutches will cost $75 more beginning three months from now, tell your customers this to help them decide to have them built now rather than waiting. Of course, if you're already too busy, you may want to change your price right now.

Regional Pricing

One more aspect of pricing your woodworking that you should consider before we get into pricing specific products is regional pricing. The price you should expect for hand-carved wooden chests in suburban Chicago is higher than the price you'll get in rural Alabama. Why? Many reasons.

First, folks in urban and suburban areas will probably have more discretionary income, or money they can spend on the finer things of life, than people living in rural areas. Second, the cost of materials may be higher in the big city. Third, the cost of labor is typically higher in the city; it costs more to live and work there. Fourth, rural areas are more likely to have native craftspeople who will compete with you.

Factoring in Regional Differences

How much of a factor is region in pricing? Overall, craft prices are about 10 percent less in rural areas than they are in medium-size cities, and about 5 to 10 percent more in metropolitan areas. Some areas where economic conditions are lower will have craft prices about 20 percent less

than medium-size cities.

So a 30 percent difference in prices is possible for the same woodworking product between suburban Chicago and rural towns. Actually, the price difference can be even more — or less — depending on other factors. But these approximations can help you in setting a shop rate and unit price for your woodworking depending on where you sell your products.

Remember that this regional price difference is based on where the products are sold, not where they are made. That's why many woodworkers in rural areas try to sell their products in larger cities. Life isn't necessarily any better or worse in any of these regions. People are simply more prepared to pay higher prices in some locations than they are in others. The smart woodworker will consider these regional pricing differences in selling his or her products.

That's the craft of pricing. Of course, there's much more to know about pricing your woodworking. The next three chapters offer specifics on pricing crafts, folk art, woodcarving, woodturning, furniture, cabinetry, and other popular woodworking crafts. Then I'll show you how to increase your profits without reducing quality. Finally, you'll see how to use technology to price, market and sell more of your great woodworking products.

TWO

Pricing Crafts *and* Folk Art

Many woodworkers begin their part-time business venture by selling crafts and folk art: toys, games, birdhouses, whirligigs, frames, clocks, lamps, boxes, kitchen tools and desk accessories. Why? Because these items have a large market and they require less of an investment than other woodworking products. In addition, they help woodworkers develop skills while paying for their equipment and time.

Pricing of crafts and folk art is also more structured than other types of woodworking products. Prices charged for whirligigs at a craft fair, for example, usually vary by no more than 20 percent between vendors — even with varied quality. One reason is that craft fairs typically have more woodworkers selling wood craft and folk art items than selling any other type of woodworking product. The competition tends to equalize prices.

Basics of Pricing Wood Crafts and Folk Art

How can you ensure that you get the best price for your crafts and folk art? As discussed in chapter one, you can learn exactly what each product costs you to make and sell. You can also make sure your pricing is competitive with other woodworkers with whom you will compete. Most important, you can ensure that you sell value over price.

Let's consider these factors as you develop prices for your wood crafts: how to cost materials, how to set labor fees, how to estimate overhead, how to set your profit and how to sell value.

Costing Materials

Materials for most crafts and folk art items are simpler and less expensive than other woodworking products. Components tend to be smaller, often of less-expensive softwoods and fewer in number.

This makes estimating the cost of materials much easier.

As many of the products in this category are produced in quantity — such as a dozen birdhouses at one time — the costs are further reduced. You typically have less scrap and more efficient use of your time. You can also buy your materials in larger quantities at lower costs.

Setting Shop Rates

Producing wood crafts requires only basic woodworking skills. That's why it's an excellent starting point for your woodworking venture. Even if you have advanced skills, you may not feel ready to use them productively to make more creative products. You may feel more comfortable making birdhouses or toys.

Of course, you will be paid for the skills you use rather than those you know. Even if you're an accomplished carver, cutting out puzzle parts with a band saw won't use your carving skills and you won't be paid for them. Nor will you need specialized tools for most craft products.

Many woodworkers who produce craft items or folk art establish a shop rate on the lower side of the spectrum. The typical shop rate for this category is $35 to $45 per hour. The lower rate is for products that can easily be mass-produced using one or two shop tools and minimal finish work. The higher rate goes for higher skills used to finish these products. A whirligig, for example, requires cutting and sanding of parts: basic skills. But it also requires assembly, sometimes involving complicated mechanisms, and painting. Much of the value of the end product depends on your assembly and painting skills. So a complex whirligig design with lifelike features can not only command a higher price, it can also earn the maker a higher hourly shop rate.

Estimating Overhead

How much you allow for overhead depends on the number of tools required to produce your woodworking crafts and folk art. Typical tools include a table saw, radial-arm saw, band saw, drill press, portable drill, router, circular saw and sander. Common hand tools include measuring devices, squares, calipers, hand files, rasps, claw hammer, mallet, pliers and clamps. You may have other tools you use for specific projects, such as socket wrenches to assemble whirligigs or corner clamps for frames.

Ensuring Profit

How can you ensure that you make a fair profit from selling your woodworking crafts and folk art? By building your profit into your markup. Many basic woodworking products are marked up 50 percent from their cost for wholesale sales. That is, a mantel clock that costs you $30 to produce (including materials, clock mechanism, labor and overhead) should be priced at about $45 to wholesale buyers. If you sell directly to customers, you have additional sales costs and you can double the wholesale cost, offering it for about $90.

If you sell the product directly to the end user, you should increase the price slightly to allow for negotiation without cutting into your profits. In the example of the clock, setting the price at $100 allows you to discount the price by 10 percent ($10) and still ensure a fair profit. If you don't expect to give a discount very often, you can lower the price to one that is more standard — such as $89.95 — and still make sure you get your standard profit.

Selling Value

In the more competitive fields of crafts and folk art, selling value over price will help you compete with other woodworkers without having to resort to deep price cutting. Chapter one discusses many ways you can sell value over price.

What is the value of your product? Make a list of the features and benefits that your woodworking product gives customers. For example, a wooden toy truck's value will include:

- Sturdy construction (feature) to last many generations (benefit)
- Hand-painted cab (feature) for a realistic look (benefit)
- Unique design (feature) that will be treasured for many years (benefit)

Remember, whenever price is discussed, take the opportunity to sell value. Don't assume that the customer sees all the features and recognizes the benefits of purchasing your woodworking product instead of someone else's. Point them out.

Toys and Games

One of the most popular categories of woodworking products you can sell is toys and games for children and adults. Toys include cars and trucks, puzzles and games, construction toys, riding toys, dollhouses and many others. Woodworkers have also successfully made and sold wooden trains, wagons, riding toys, hobbyhorses, pull toys, action toys, wooden locks and even executive or desk toys.

Wooden toys and games require a minimal investment in stock. In fact, some woodworkers build these products out of the scrap from making furniture, cabinets and other larger projects. Or they collect the scrap from other woodworkers. Because making wooden toys and games is such an easy field to get into, competition is often high. However, most of your competitors may be making wooden trucks or jigsaw puzzles or some other product. If you find a unique design and add value to it, your products will face minimal competition.

Shop Rate

Many designs are available that can be constructed in a short time while offering the woodworker a fair shop rate. A shop rate of $35 to $55 an hour is typical, depending on the uniqueness of the design and the efficiency of the shop. Because making toys requires a higher investment in labor than other woodworking products, the markup is typically higher. Many toys and games are priced at four times the cost of materials. Of course, if your materials are free, estimate the cost to purchase these materials through normal channels.

Pricing

Wooden cars and trucks are frequently priced between $12 and $35 each, depending on complexity and the amount of time required for construction. That means materials should cost between $3 and about $8 per unit. The more labor required to build your product, the higher the multiplier. Construction toys, like building blocks, are sold in sets commonly priced between $25 and $45 for the set. Larger and smaller sets can be offered to meet customer's pocketbooks and local competition.

Riding toys have a smaller market as they are limited to users between the ages of about two and six years. Designs include wagons, airplanes, tractors, hobbyhorses, rocking horses and walking or pedal cars. Depending on complexity, materials, finish and uniqueness, wooden riding toys often sell for $60 and up. Few designs are priced above $250. Of course, designs, materials and craftsmanship vary so much that you can often set your own price. If possible, stay away from designs that are similar to riding toys purchased at toy shops. The more competition, the more difficult it is to get your price.

Carousel horses are a separate category. They are not really toys, nor are they intended to be ridden. And in most cases, they are hand-carved rather than produced with saw blades. However, if you've selected carousel horses as your woodwork-

ing product, they should sell from $200 to $3,000 each. Materials are only a small component of the price, and carousel horse woodworkers use pricing multipliers of 5 to 20. For more information on carousel horses, subscribe to *The Carousel News & Trader* (87 Park Avenue West, Suite 206, Mansfield, OH 44902; www.carouseltrader.com).

To reduce production costs for wooden toys and games, you can purchase some components through woodworking supply catalogs. They offer wooden toy wheels and axles, toy train parts and even kits that require only finishing. These suppliers also sell plans for popular toy and game projects. Of course, if they are so popular, you will face more competition, so try to make your product unique.

Birdhouses

If you have limited woodworking tools and experience, wooden birdhouses are an excellent entry-level product. They can be constructed of inexpensive materials using basic tools, and they are very popular. This also means the competition will be higher, minimizing profits. However, if you can develop a unique design or a simplified method of construction, you can ensure that birdhouses are both profitable and fun.

Pricing

Pricing birdhouses is difficult. Simple birdhouses of cedar can be sold for as little as $20, while ornate bird condominiums with hand-painting will sell for $200 or more. A shop rate of $30 to $45 per hour is typical for birdhouse builders. They often multiply material costs by three to arrive at a retail price, or by two for a wholesale price. That is, a birdhouse that requires $15 in materials is typically sold to a wholesaler for about $30, or directly to the customer for $45. The wholesaler will probably mark up the birdhouse twice and sell it for $60. So, in this example, you can set your retail price between $45 and $60, depending on how you sell it, how much it costs you to sell it and what your competitors charge.

One way of getting a higher price for your birdhouses is to develop a unique design or one that simulates an antique design. A unique design would be a birdhouse that looks like the White House, your state's capitol building or your city's municipal offices. Or you can copy a birdhouse design from an old Sears or Wards catalog. The less your woodworking product looks like your competitors' products, the higher you can price it.

Selling Related Items

Some birdhouse builders also make and sell bird feeders and birdbaths. Customers interested in birdhouses may also buy these products at the same time, increasing your income and reducing your selling costs. Or you can make and sell wooden birdcages of either modern or Victorian design. Shop rate and multiplier on these woodworking products are the same as for birdhouses.

Whirligigs

Whirligigs are an American tradition dating back to the beginning of our country. At the end of the Revolution, George Washington brought some "whilagigs" in his saddle bags for Martha's grandchildren. "The Legend of Sleepy Hollow" by Washington Irving refers to these wind toys. Whirligigs are mechanical toys, usually made of wood, that harness wind power to perform some action. Nonmechanical whirligigs are similar to weather vanes. Because whirligigs require more labor than many other woodworking products, they are typically priced at a higher multiple of material costs. In many cases, the multiple is four

times material costs. That is, a whirligig that requires $7 worth of materials should retail for about $28. Depending on the complexity of the design and the labor involved, even five times the cost is reasonable.

Antique whirligigs are quite expensive, ranging in price from $500 to over $2,500 for some designs. Reproductions can be made from these designs, or new designs can be developed. Moving-torso, single-arm and double-arm whirligigs are typically priced between $25 and $50 each. More complex whirligigs, such as hidden shaft and double cam designs, are higher, ranging from $40 to $80 or more. Some woodcrafters sell their whirligigs for $100 or more by patterning them after antique designs and giving them an antique-look finish.

Numerous books are available on whirligig design and construction. Anders S. "Andy" Lunde is one of the best-known authors in this specialty with a number of books on the whirligig design and construction. One of the best is *Whirligigs in Silhouette* (Modern Handcraft, 1989). This book includes 25 patterns for mechanical and nonmechanical whirligigs along with step-by-step instructions on how to build them.

Picture Frames

Making and selling wooden picture frames is a lucrative business, especially if you can find a niche that allows you to develop a market of repeat customers. Some picture-frame makers sell directly to the public, framing art or other items for display. Some manufacture frames for resale by others either as components (such as in a frame shop) or as part of an artistic product (such as in an art gallery).

Frames are labor-intensive. The basic frame stock may go through six or more operations before becoming the final product. Each operation may require a new setup. Finished frames will then sell from $35 to as much as $500 each, depending on size, design, finish and "value." As with other woodworking products, the more unique the design, the higher the perceived value and the eventual price.

Shop Rate

Making frames requires advanced woodworking skills and tools for higher shop rates, but can be started with basic tools and skills while the trade is learned. Picture-frame makers establish shop rates of $40 to $50 an hour for jobs requiring only basic tools and skills, moving up to $55 or $60 an hour for custom frame production. Some frame craftspeople earn as much as $65 an hour for their shop rate.

Another way of establishing your frames as unique is to utilize woods that are not as common. One successful frame maker uses myrtle wood, an evergreen with a fine grain, to make unique frames. Others use regional hardwoods, selling them in markets where such woods are difficult to find.

Clocks

A clock typically isn't made of wood, but many clock mechanisms are installed in wood cases or frames. Woodworkers can make a wide variety of clock cases, including grandfather, grandmother (slightly shorter than a grandfather clock), wall, regulator, shelf, mantel, ship, marine and schoolhouse. Some woodworkers simply add a quartz clock movement to a woodworking product such as a picture frame, a wall plaque or a wooden toy. Others build elaborate cases with beveled or leaded glass or with exotic wood panels. Still other woodworkers build wood cases and frames for weather instruments such as barometers and thermometers. *Woodshop News'* survey of craft shops lists clocks fifth in popularity of 20 wood craft products.

Pricing

Pricing simple clocks is easier than many other woodworking products because so many woodworkers are making clocks. Customers have lots of competitive products to look at. For that reason, retail prices and hourly shop rates can be lower than might be earned with the skills required to build ornate clocks. For example, it may be difficult to earn a shop rate of $45 to $55 an hour appropriate for advanced skills and equipment necessary to build an oak clock case. The resulting clock may have a manufacturing cost that requires a retail price of $2,500, yet it must compete with clocks that competitors are mass-producing for sale at $1,500 each. The answer for some clock woodworkers is to lower their shop rate from $45 an hour to $40 an hour. Others develop a unique design that cannot easily be compared with competitors' clocks. Still others sell only through channels that don't expect a quality clock for $1,200.

Of course, clock prices vary from $15 for a quartz wall clock to over $4,000 for a hand-carved freestanding clock with elaborate movement. The materials cost, skill levels and time required also vary greatly. As a guideline, many woodworkers establish a shop rate of $35 to $45 for simple clocks and $45 to $55 for clocks that require more skill, experience and tools to produce. A simple wall clock may require only $5 for materials and a half hour's labor. A carved or turned clock case may require 100 hours of labor and an expensive movement.

An Atypical Markup

Because clocks require time mechanisms and other nonwood components, the markup or multiplier isn't the same as for other woodworking products. As a rule of thumb, multiply wood material costs by three to four (depending on how much detail work is required) and multiply mechanism and glass materials by two. For example, a mantel clock that requires $30 in wood and finishing materials

(× 3 or 4) plus a $40 clock mechanism (× 2) is typically priced at $170 to $200. Depending on competition, uniqueness of design, region where it is sold and your selling ability, the example clock may be retailed at $120 to $200.

Some woodworkers with limited tools start making and selling clocks by purchasing and finishing clock kits. This requires little more than a workbench, a few tools, finishing materials and some time. As a rule of thumb, material costs can be multiplied by two to arrive at a probable retail price. A $150 regulator clock kit can typically be assembled, finished and sold for about $300.

Pricing Examples
Grandfather clocks retail from about $2,500 to $6,000 each, with the movement costing between $600 and $2,000. Wall clocks are priced between $300 and $1,000 each, with movements costing $100 to $300. Mantel clocks typically retail for about the same price as wall clocks with the movements approximately as expensive. Movements and kits can be purchased from Emperor Clock Co. (PO Box 1089, Fairhope, AL 36533; www.emperorclock.com) and Klockit (PO Box 636, N3211 County Road H, Lake Geneva, WI 53147; www.klockit.com). In Canada, contact Murray Clock Craft (512 McNicholl Avenue, Willowdale, ON M4H 2E1; www.murrayclock.com).

Remember that these are only guidelines and rules of thumb. Much depends on the customer's perception of value. Does it look like a $300 clock, or is it similar to a Wal-Mart clock that sells for $79.95? The more unique you can make your woodworking product, the greater the perceived value — and the higher the price you can get.

Lamps

Lamps come in all sizes, shapes and types. Turned lamps will be priced in chapter three. Here, we will price wooden lamps constructed using saws, routers and related tools.

Lamps offer the same advantage/disadvantage in pricing that many other woodworking products have: They can be purchased anywhere. The ornate table lamp that you've spent many hours making and finishing is similar in function and general design to others available at the local lighting shop or discount store. So you must find and emphasize the unique qualities of your lamps in order to earn a higher price for them.

Shop Rate
As most wooden lamps require only basic woodworking skills to produce, the shop rate for making them is on the low side of the scale: $35 to $45 an hour. A common multiplier is three times material costs for woodworking components and two times material costs for electrical components and shades. So a lamp that requires $25 in wood and finishing materials (× 3) and $30 for wiring and a shade (× 2) will be priced at about $135. Using this guideline, you should be spending no more than one hour making the lamp from wood and less than an hour assembling the unit to earn the suggested shop rate. You probably won't earn this shop rate on the first unit or two you make, but should once you've done a few.

If you choose to make lamps for profit, decide how you will sell them and look at what the competition is doing. If you plan to sell them wholesale to furniture stores and lighting shops, talk with store buyers about their needs. Remember that many furniture stores mark up their products by a multiplier of two or three. So a lamp that you sell wholesale for $80 will retail at a furniture store for $160 to $240. The buyer at a local store can tell you what price range sells best, and you can then decide whether or not you can sell your lamps wholesale and still make a reasonable profit.

Wooden Boxes

The *Woodshop News* survey of craft shops nationwide reported that wooden boxes and jewelry boxes are their most popular wood craft products. You can make and sell numerous types of wooden boxes, including music boxes, jewelry boxes, oval boxes, sculptured boxes, hand-carved-lid boxes, nesting boxes, jigsaw boxes or larger boxes such as cedar hope chests and toy chests.

Pricing

How can you price wooden boxes? First, determine what they cost you to make, using your established shop rate. Rates for woodworkers making wooden boxes typically range from $35 to $50 an hour. Rather than size, it is uniqueness that sets a higher hourly rate. That's because unique products have less competition. If your customer has seen a similar toy chest at Sears for $100, you will have difficulty getting $300 for yours — and in receiving a fair shop rate. Make your design unique and then be sure to show the customer how your product is more valuable than the competition's.

Small wooden boxes offer an opportunity for advanced craftsmanship in design, construction and finishing. The selection of design and materials is important and can earn you a higher price for your work. A simple design and finish may be priced as low as $20 and will rarely earn a reasonable return for the craftsperson. But by making the design unique, you can sell the box for $50 or more with little additional effort.

Larger wooden boxes, too, can earn a higher price by making them unique. Hundreds of cedar chests look and are priced similarly to each other.

But by adding a carving to the inlaying on the top, or using a more exotic wood, you can enhance the uniqueness — and ultimately the value — of the chest.

Copying Antique Designs

One method of developing unique wooden box designs is to copy from the past. That is, check antique and collectible shops for a box that stands out and can be built with your tools and skills, then copy it. You may find a pantry box or a candle box that you like and develop a similar design. In any case, the more unusual and interesting the design (and the more it doesn't look like your competition's), the more you can get for it.

Kitchen Tools and Accessories

You can get tremendous satisfaction in making kitchen tools and accessories for others because you know that they will be used frequently. A spice cabinet you make may be opened and admired every day for many years. This is one reason why many woodworkers choose to make and sell kitchen items. Another reason is that they sell easily. A survey of craft shops conducted by *Woodshop News* indicated that kitchen accessories came in third in popularity with customers.

Many tools and accessories can be or are made of wood. They include cooking utensils, towel drying stands, spice cabinets, corner shelves, step stools, lazy Susans, wine racks, wineglass holders, spoon racks, knife holders, napkin holders, cutting boards, coaster sets, dough boxes and related items. Most kitchen tools and accessories are small and can easily be mass-produced. Of course, you will want to make your design unique so you can get top dollar.

Shop Rate

The shop rate for a kitchen-accessory maker is typically in the medium range of $35 to $55 an hour. Why? The skill level for making these items is about the same as many other woodworking products, but the market is bigger and more receptive. Unique wooden kitchen accessories make great wedding, housewarming, holiday and birthday gifts. If prices are under $50, they are often an impulse buy: "I think Judy would love to have one of these."

Selling Related Items

Another advantage to making and selling kitchen tools and accessories is that people frequently buy more than one item at a time. If you sell a knife block to a customer, you may also be able to sell a set of wooden spoons, a cutting board or related items. This increases the total amount of the sale, reduces your marketing costs, and gives you the opportunity for a higher income.

Tools

If you are in love with tools, especially old-fashioned wooden tools used by your grandfather, consider making reproductions of these tools for others. It may not pay as well financially as other forms of woodworking, but it can pay high dividends of satisfaction.

Tools include wooden wheelbarrows, felling axes, mallets, hay rakes, planes, broad axes, seed dryers, and related items. One successful woodworker purchased old tools, replaced the wooden components, cleaned up the metal parts and resold them as "remodeled antiques."

Shop Rate

The typical shop rate for making or repairing wooden tools is $30 to $45 an hour. To increase the shop rate, some woodworkers specialize in a specific type of tool and market their product to a defined group of customers. For example, a Midwest woodworker makes wooden planes used in many historic community shops. By specializing, he has established a shop rate of $45 an hour for his work.

For more information on antique tools, read the *Fine Tool Journal* (27 Fickett Road, Pownal, ME 04069; www.finetoolj.com).

Desk Accessories

Many woodworkers overlook desk accessories as an opportunity — which is exactly why you should consider them. Desk accessories include pens, pen holders, letter openers, bookends, award plaques, "executive toys," bookshelves, blackboards and message boards, and computer accessories. Because few woodworkers make these products, you can earn a higher hourly shop rate and sell items more easily.

The *Woodshop News* survey of craft shops across the nation reported that desk accessories are the sixth most popular wood craft products they sell.

Shop Rate

Hourly shop rates for making desk accessories are often higher than other woodworking products, ranging from $45 to $55 an hour depending on the skill of the craftsperson and the uniqueness of the design. Woodworking products sold to businesses typically earn a higher price than those sold to the general public. Why? Even though the businesses don't resell your product, they do gain a nonmonetary profit. An employer gets a more efficient or more satisfied worker or a happier customer. You get a better price.

Finding a Market

The key to selling desk accessories is finding the right market. Rather than selling through traditional methods, one enterprising woodworker developed a plaque design that reproduced a signature. He then sold these unique nameplates as gifts that companies could give to employees who had worked at their firms for five years. Employers purchased them for $70 each and gave them to employees in recognition of service. He also developed a more decorative version for gifts at 10 and 15 years of service as well as low-cost wooden plaques for other employees.

Miniatures

If you have the tools — and the patience — to make wooden miniatures, you can earn a higher shop rate for your work. Miniatures include dollhouse furniture and similar items. Miniatures are typically replicas of larger woodworking products scaled to less than one-half original size. You can specialize in miniature period furniture, miniatures of a specific item such as kitchen appliances or rocking chairs, or custom miniatures for the film industry or other nontypical clients.

Shop Rate

Depending on skills, tools and market, the shop rate for a miniatures craftsperson will range from $40 to $65 an hour. That's a broad range because the market is broad. Some woodworkers make miniatures that are difficult to distinguish from dollhouse furniture found at most toy stores, while others make unique items that attract upscale buyers. Also, much depends on your investment in tools. Power tools for miniature woodworking are not as expensive as standard tools, but they are still expensive. You also need more of them. On the plus side, you can set up a woodworking shop for

miniatures in a spare room or shed rather than take over half of the garage.

Other Crafts and Folk Art

You can make and sell many other woodworking crafts and folk art products. They include wooden baskets, walking canes, farm tool reproductions, musical instruments, wooden wheelbarrows, old-fashioned hand tools, folding candleholders and crystal window decorations. How can you profitably price them to sell? Apply the rules of pricing outlined in chapter one and verified in this chapter.

Shop Rate

Woodworking products that require fewer skills, tools and materials will earn lower shop rates of $35 to $45 an hour. Advanced skills and designs can earn $45 to $55 an hour. A few unique items where the craftsperson is well known will earn $55 to $65 an hour for the woodworker.

As discussed in chapter one, other factors to consider are your needs, the local economy, the competition, and how hungry you are for the sale. You've also learned that by finding the best market and by selling value rather than price, you can earn higher hourly shop rates for your skills.

Other woodworkers have successfully — and profitably — sold crafts and folk art. So can you!

CHAPTER

THREE

Pricing Woodcarving *and* Woodturning

Woodcarvings and turnings are labor-intensive products where it seems that the woodworker is paid by the amount of shavings on the floor.

Woodcarving and woodturning are creative skills that require years to develop and demand specialized tools. They also command a higher hourly rate than making common craft items. If you have these skills and tools, you can be paid well for them by learning how to price your products. That's what this chapter is all about.

Basics of Pricing Woodcarving

Unfortunately, many woodcarvers give their products away with a labor rate of just a few dollars an hour. Of course, the customer will normally not pay you more than you ask for your carvings. The customer depends on you to determine the value of your work. If you ask only $10 for a fine piece, that's all you'll get. As discussed in chapter one, if you ask for $50 and explain its value to the customer, that's probably what you'll get. You must learn to set a reasonable price that gives you a fair hourly wage yet stays within the range of what a customer can be persuaded to pay. In this chapter, you'll learn how to price woodcarvings and turnings. This first section is on carvings: how to cost materials, set labor fees, estimate overhead, ensure a profit and sell value. You'll also learn what other woodcarvers charge for their labor and products.

One excellent way of learning what others are charging for their woodcarvings is to join an association like the National Wood Carvers Association (PO Box 43218, Cincinnati, OH 45243; www.chipchats.org). The reasonable membership dues include a subscription to the bimonthly *Chip Chats* magazine. The NWCA has members throughout the world.

Costing Materials

Woodcarvers typically buy fewer materials than other woodworkers, and the woods tend to be softer and less expensive, so estimating the cost of materials is relatively easy once a stable supplier is found. Rather than purchase numerous components, a woodcarver uses a single piece or blank for each carving. Blanks can be purchased in quantity to reduce costs.

Setting Shop Rates

Shop rates for woodcarvers are typically from $35 to $55 an hour depending on many factors: skill, talent, tools and originality. A whittler who carves identical figurines with basic tools may earn only $35 or $40 an hour. A woodworker who carves unique birds or mammals for galleries may set an hourly rate of $50 or even $60. Most carvers will set an hourly rate somewhere in between, depending on skills, experience and uniqueness of their designs.

Again, much depends on the tools that you use. A whittler needs only a few basic tools; an investment of $100 may be all that's required. Or a carver may require tools for cutting his or her own blanks and preparing them for the final carving process. The investment in tools may be $1,000 or more. This is part of your woodworking venture's overhead and thus a component of your shop rate or labor fees.

Estimating Overhead

Your overhead costs for woodcarving and turning relate to the amount and cost of tools you need to perform your craft. Typical tools for woodcarving include hand tools such as whittling knives, gouges, chisels, measuring and marking devices, squares, calipers, hand files, rasps, claw hammer, mallet, pliers and clamps, as well as a grinding wheel, grinding tools, table saw, radial-arm saw and band saw. Some carvers also have a drill press, portable drill, router, circular saw, miter saw and sander. By tracking the cost of tools and how long you expect them to last, you can determine their value to you. You may establish that your tools are minimal and cost you only $5 an hour for purchase, maintenance, sharpening and replacement. That's $5 for each hour you use them. Or you may have a band saw for cutting out blanks, estimating that it adds another $3 an hour to your overhead. In any case, you must know how much your tools cost you in order to set your fees and to ensure you have money to repair or replace these tools when the time comes.

Ensuring Profit

Because woodcarving is such a labor-intensive craft, multipliers and mark-ups are somewhat different from other woodworking products. The stock may cost only 10 percent of the wholesale price of the finished item — $5 for a blank that will become a product priced at $50 wholesale or $100 retail. Tools and related overhead may add another 5 percent of wholesale. The labor may be about three-quarters of the wholesale price. The example of a $100 retail item may require an hour to produce at a $35-an-hour shop rate. The cost is now $42 ($5 + $2.50 + $35 = $42.50). A $46.75 wholesale price will allow for a profit of 10 percent of wholesale, or $4.25. In this example, percentages would be:

	% OF WHOLESALE	% OF RETAIL
Materials	10	5
Overhead	5	2.5
Labor	75	37.5
Profit	10	5
Sales Costs	___	50
Total	100%	100%

Selling Value

Value is the worth of something, often measured in dollars. Value is established in the mind of the buyer depending on how he or she sees the product's usefulness and importance. Value is also established by comparing the product's benefits to those of similar products.

So you can see what you need to do to sell the value of your wood carvings: Help the buyer understand the product's usefulness and importance. That is, sell him or her on the benefits. For example:

- "This is a one-of-a-kind carving of a cowboy I once met in Montana. There are no other carvings like it in the world."
- "Your friends will admire the detail of the figure's craggy face and realistic attire."
- "This is an exact replica of the Point Reyes lighthouse just a few miles from here. It will be a lifetime souvenir of your stay on the California coast."

Help the buyer see the value of your work and you will sell more.

Carved Figures and Scenes

One broad category of woodworking covers everything from whittling cowboy figures to carving ornate murals. What these carved figures and scenes have in common is that all are done with basic carving tools, few of them power tools. In fact, the investment in tools for this type of woodworking can be as little as $100.

Because so much of carving requires handwork, it is labor-intensive. That is, the labor factor of your price is higher than other woodworking and your overhead factor (tools, shop costs, etc.) is lower.

Pricing

These variables make pricing some carved products more challenging. Until you have experience, it is difficult to estimate how much time it will take to create a carved figure from a piece of wood. Multiplying the cost of materials doesn't work because materials are a smaller percentage of the total investment. Some carvers break the project down into stages and can better estimate the time required for each stage. For some carvings, the rough carving or initial carving can be done quickly; for others, the rough is more than half the job. Keeping track of your time by task takes just a few moments and can reward you with more accurate pricing.

Because tools are less expensive, a carver's shop rate depends more on his or her skills and experience. An efficient carver can establish a shop rate of $45 an hour, but most start at about $35 to $40 an hour. A simple carving can often be completed by skilled hands in a half hour, though many take two to six hours. Larger carvings such as murals and signs require a minimum of four hours to complete, with some commissions needing as many as 100 hours. Much depends on your skills, your productivity and the perceived value of your product.

Carved Decoys

The carving of decoys is a subset of carving figures, discussed above. However, it is also an industry unto itself with world-renowned craftspeople who carve nothing else. Similar to carving decoys is carving other wildlife figures such as birds and mammals. While cowboys and scenes allow the craftsperson to carve caricatures, decoys and wildlife carvings replicate the original to a fine degree. Decoys and wildlife carvings look like the real thing.

Shop Rate

Because carving decoys and wildlife requires artistry as well as craftsmanship, carvers typically earn a higher shop rate. They also often use miniature power tools to reduce hand work. These tools add to the cost of overhead. The shop rate for carving decoys and wildlife ranges from $40 to $50 an hour depending on skills, tools and artistic abilities. Many experienced decoy and wildlife carvers set their shop rate at $50 an hour. Others start at $40 an hour and increase it by 10 percent an hour each year until they reach their target shop rate.

Specializing

Some decoy carvers model their work after designs from the past. They find a photo or actual carving they like and reproduce it. As antique decoys bring prices between $75 and $2,000, replicating a unique design can often earn a higher price than copying a current design. Of course, you should identify your product as a replica of an original.

One successful decoy carver developed a second line of miniature decoys that he could easily produce and offer at less than half the price of his full-size decoys. In fact, his hourly rate for the miniatures is slightly higher than for his larger decoys. Best of all, he is offering a product that he can sell to those who want a representation of his work but can't afford his standard decoys. He has also used the miniatures as a promotional piece, giving one away in a drawing at shows he attends. He figures people who sign up for the drawing are potential clients for his products and puts them on his mailing list. (More about mailing lists in chapter five.)

Chain-Saw Art

At the other end of the spectrum is chain-saw art. Woodworkers use smaller, lighter chain saws to carve and detail chunks of wood into recognizable objects. One successful chain-saw artist in a tourist area has set up a walk-through park where he displays his work — for an admission charge. Along the paths are chain-saw bears, cougars, rabbits and other critters. He has also set up a Western town with chain-saw cowboys lounging on the porch and in the saloon. He has a shop where he demonstrates and sells his crafts as well.

Shop Rate

Your shop rate for chain-saw art may range from $35 to $50 an hour, depending on skills, local interest and competition. Because overhead is lower (you need only one or two chain saws), hourly shop rates are lower. In fact, one successful chain-saw artist sets up each weekend at a flea market and fires up his chain saw to draw customers. He has no shop. All materials and finished products are in his utility trailer. The higher hourly rate goes for commissioned work where a customer asks the craftsperson to carve a specific figure.

Basics of Pricing Woodturning

Woodturning is typically a leisurely task that invites novice woodworkers with its old-world image and the smells of freshly cut wood. Because wood can be turned into so many unique shapes, it is also an excellent opportunity for expressing your creativity. The problem is that many woodturners put more time into their products than they can ever get out of them. They must learn to produce turnings efficiently while making unique designs that sell themselves.

Let's look at how other woodturners cost materials, set labor fees, estimate overhead, ensure profit and sell value.

Costing Materials

Turning crafters typically buy fewer materials than other woodworkers, but they often buy unique woods that cost more. Woods tend to be more exotic and more expensive. Even so, estimating the cost of materials is relatively easy once a stable supplier is found. Rather than purchase numerous components, a woodturner will work with one or two pieces or blanks per product.

Fortunately, if the craftsperson has selected a single type of product to produce, blanks can be purchased in quantity to reduce costs. Of course, the craftsperson doesn't want to tie up all profits in raw materials, but markup is sufficient to allow profits that can purchase materials well in advance of need and earn a discount on materials.

Setting Shop Rates

Shop rates for woodturners are typically from $40 to $55 an hour, depending on skill, talent, tools and originality. A turner making identical bowls with basic tools may earn only $40 or $45 an hour. A woodworker who turns unique bowls out of exotic woods for galleries may earn an hourly rate of $50 to $55 or more.

As with other woodworking, your shop rate depends on the tools you use. One turner may use a simple lathe and basic tools valued at less than $500. Another turner may require special tools costing $3,000 or more for production. The cost of tools is part of your shop's overhead and must be included in your shop rate or labor fees.

Estimating Overhead

Typical tools for woodturning include a lathe, grinding wheel and tools, table saw, radial-arm saw, band saw, drill press, portable drill and possibly a router. Common hand tools include turning chisels, measuring and marking devices, squares, calipers, hand files, rasps, claw hammer, mallet, pliers and clamps. You may need other tools for specific projects, such as spray equipment for finishing larger turnings.

Ensuring Profit

Like woodcarving, turning is a labor-intensive craft. Pricing and profits are different from other woodworking products. Woodturners spend more on materials and tools/overhead than do woodcarvers. The price of a typical woodturning product will break down like this:

	% OF WHOLESALE	% OF RETAIL
Materials	20	10
Overhead	10	5
Labor	60	30
Profit	10	5
Sales Costs		50
Total	100%	100%

For example, a bowl for which the blank costs $15 will typically become a finished product that will wholesale for $75 or retail for $150. In this example, about $45 will be charged to labor (60 percent of $75 wholesale, or 30 percent of $150 retail). The shop rate includes overhead, labor and profit, or $60 in the example (80 percent of $75 wholesale, or 40 percent of $150 retail). If your shop rate is $50 an hour, that means you should be spending about 50 minutes producing this product. If you're spending more, review your price or your production methods. This time estimate is for efficient production, not leisurely hobby time.

Selling Value

Value is the worth of a product or service. Price is the amount of money given by the buyer in exchange for value. To increase the price, increase the value or make sure that the buyer recognizes the value of the product. Why wouldn't the typical buyer pay $500 for a turned candlesticks? Because the buyer doesn't believe the value is $500.

How can you sell the value of your woodturnings? One way of doing so, as discussed in chapter one is to answer price questions with points of value:

- "Yes, that bowl is priced at $250 because it is a one-of-a-kind item that combines many hours of work and many years of skill. You'll remember the quality long after you've forgotten the price."
- "Of course, Wal-Mart has some candleholders for $4 each. These candleholders will outlast Wal-Mart's by many years, yet won't look like everyone else's."
- "$400 does seem like a lot of money for a figurine. Each figure I sculpt comes from hand-selected timber and takes advantage of the natural personality of the wood. You won't go into someone else's house and see a figurine like yours. And I finish each piece by hand to ensure that your figurine will look this good for many years."

Candlesticks

A century ago, candles were a practical requirement of everyday life. Candlesticks were just as practical. Today, candles and candlesticks are decorative products that accent a table or a room. Wooden candlesticks offer woodturners an opportunity for creative expression — and profit.

Candlesticks range in size from 1" or 2" high to ornate candle stands up to 4' tall. Some are turned from a single blank, while others require five or six individually turned pieces that are then assembled.

Pricing

Once designs are selected, candlesticks can be produced in quantity, reducing the cost per unit. A woodturner who produces candlesticks typically has about six designs from which the customer can choose. That number of designs offers the customer sufficient choices without making the decision too difficult. It can also offer a wide field of prices so that each customer finds something in his or her price range.

Shop Rate

Woodturners who produce candlesticks and related items typically establish a shop rate of $40 to $50 an hour, depending on skills, tools, designs, creativity and ability to sell value. Producing multiple units during the same work session reduces the cost per unit and allows the woodworker to maintain competitive prices. More than many other types of woodworking, candlesticks compete with products found in large retail stores. Also, because many beginning woodturners start with candlesticks, the experienced craftsperson must increase efficiency to compete with the beginner's lower shop rate.

Turned Bowls

Wooden bowls can be placed in one of two broad categories: mostly functional or mostly artistic. In the mostly functional category are the wooden bowls that can be used for displaying fruit, flowers or other decorations. They might even be used as everyday bowls. Artistic wooden bowls are quite different. You would never consider placing food in an artistic wooden bowl — especially one that cost $800!

The labor and craftsmanship that go into these bowls are quite different, too. A functional bowl can be produced from common stock in a short time using some automation. Artistic bowls require extensive time and skills to ensure that the best qualities of the wood are discovered and expressed in the final product. Bowl blanks from exotic woods are more expensive, too.

Shop Rate

Shop rates, as well, vary for turned bowls, depending on the end product and its use. The shop rate for producing functional bowls is typically $35 to $45 an hour, with $50 an hour charged by experienced bowl-turners. Markup is typically three to four times material costs. A blank costing $15 may become a bowl priced at $45 to $60 retail, depending on quality and finish.

Artistic bowls earn a higher shop rate because the craftsperson makes each bowl unique. Shop rates for artistic bowls range from $45 to $55 an hour, with up to $60 an hour typical for experienced artisans. With the higher shop rate comes a need to stress value over price, especially with designs that are similar to those of functional bowls. Customers for these artistic bowls are different from those who buy functional bowls, so stepping from producing one type of bowl to another means leaving many of your regular customers behind and finding new ones. Most turners who make the transition from producing functional to artistic bowls do so slowly to maintain income; the process may take more than a year to complete.

One enterprising bowl-turner traded some of his products to a craftsperson in another region who produced wooden kitchen utensils, so that each had related products to sell at craft fairs. They traded products on the basis of wholesale value: what they would sell it for to a retailer. Each then was able to make a profit on his own products as well as those for which he traded.

Turned Lamps

Using a lathe to turn lamps and lamp stands can be a profitable part-time or full-time business because people expect to pay more for lamps than they do for other woodworking products. This is an especially lucrative venture if you have a basic understanding of electricity and wiring. Even if you don't, you can purchase the electrical components and wire them according to plans found in many homeowner how-to magazines.

Pricing

Turned lamps typically retail from $50 to $300 each, earning woodworkers a shop rate of $35 to $50 an hour for their efforts. The shop rate depends on the uniqueness of the design, the craftsperson's skills and how quickly the woodworker can produce quality products. If you develop a design that is both unique and easy to manufacture, you can earn the higher shop rate. Of course, you may also be plagued by imitators who will undercut your price.

The numerous types of lamps or portable lighting include table lamps, desk lamps, study lamps, and floor lamps. Designs can be antique reproductions, classical, modern or ultramodern. Lamps can be made from standard wood stock, exotic woods or burls or can include special finishes.

How can you find a worthwhile lamp plan? The first step is to visit lamp and lighting stores in your area or in nearby cities. Tell the manager what you're doing and ask for ideas. Also ask what a particular plan would retail and wholesale for. You may even establish your first customers in this manner. With your plan in hand, visit an electrical store to determine what components you will need and their cost. Ask about wholesale prices. You may soon be making and selling turned lamps for profit.

Wooden Jewelry

Jewelry has traditionally been made of precious metals. But it can also be made from wood by the skilled craftsperson. Beads, barrettes, ornaments and even chains can be carved or turned from wood.

Shop Rate

Making wooden jewelry can earn a shop rate of $35 to $55 an hour. The wide spread is because no two craftspeople have the same skills, use the same techniques, or require the same tools. A whittler who makes wooden jewelry needs fewer tools, and the finished product will be rougher than turned jewelry, so the whittler will set a lower shop rate such as $35 to $40 an hour. The wooden-jewelry turner will need more skills and equipment, typically setting a shop rate of $45 to $55 an hour.

Pricing

Pricing individual jewelry pieces is not as difficult as it may seem. First, determine your price based on costs: materials, labor, overhead and profit. Then look at where your competitors, if any, price their products. If they aren't making the same product, how much are they getting for similar products? Then price similar jewelry made of both precious and nonprecious metals. You may discover, for example, that a hand-carved wooden brooch costs you $22 to make, that competitors are selling similar brooches for $25 to $40, and that similar metallic brooches range in price from $35 to $55. In this case, you could establish a price of about $35, especially if the design is sufficiently different from that of your competitors and you learn to sell value.

Custom Carvings and Turnings

Once you've developed a reputation as a quality craftsperson, you may be asked by customers to produce custom carvings or turnings for them. How much should you charge? That depends on many factors.

First, with experience you have probably found a shop rate that earns you sufficient wages and profit without driving too many customers away. In most cases, you can use this shop rate or an even higher one as your rate for custom work. You can typically ask for 10 to 20 percent more and get it.

For example, if your established shop rate for production work is $50 an hour, you may be able to increase that up to $55 or even $60 an hour for custom woodworking.

Should you tell your customer what your shop rate is for custom work? Normally, no. Just figure your job using the new rate. However, if you're working with professional people, such as attorneys or accountants, their "shop rate" will be even higher than yours and they will feel like they got a bargain by hiring you for less than what they get for their services. In fact, some woodcarvers and turners prefer to work exclusively with these professionals because they can get a higher shop rate for their work. They produce custom whittled or carved figures based on photos or drawings, or they make bowls or lamps to the designs of the customer.

CHAPTER

FOUR

Pricing Furniture *and* Cabinetry

One of the problems faced by craftspeople who make furniture and cabinetry is that they compete with the lumber store where they buy their stock. Even large discount stores sell wood furniture and cabinetry at prices well below the cost of quality materials and workmanship. Customers shop price.

What's the solution? Sell value!

If possible, stay away from furniture and cabinet designs that are similar to those sold at most area stores. If that isn't practical, develop a unique feature that will make your product clearly superior to other furniture or cabinets.

An enterprising bedroom-set maker had one drawer front on each piece hand-carved by a local craftsperson. The design could be selected from three stock carving designs or, for a "custom" fee, it could be nearly any design the buyers wanted. The hand carvings gave additional value to the bedroom sets and earned the furniture maker and the carver a better price.

Basics of Pricing Furniture

Pricing the furniture you make is similar to pricing any other woodworking product. You determine the cost of materials, estimate labor and overhead costs, and add in a profit so you can continue doing what you love. Some differences, of course exist, between pricing furniture and pricing desk accessories. Competition is also different. Let's consider how furniture is broadly, then specifically, priced.

Many successful furniture makers specialize in reproductions of period furniture. Common styles include Queen Anne (1720-1760), Chippendale (1755-1790), Federal (1790-1820), Victorian (1830-1890) and Art Nouveau (1880-1945). Others specialize in Shaker, Pennsylvania Dutch, primitive Country and other popular styles.

Jim Deardorff, owner of Out of the Woods Furniture Co., produces rustic furniture from alder, selling through art furniture galleries. He specializes in rocking chairs and related tables. "I found that I couldn't compete with the larger shops that mass-produced rocking chairs on an assembly line, so I decided to specialize in high quality to an elite customer." Rustic furniture retains the bark on many components. Jim uses dowels rather than screws and hand-selects all woods. The chairs retail for $1,500 to $2,000 each. He sells them wholesale to galleries for about half the retail price. Jim's advice to furniture makers pricing their work is, "Don't quit your day job yet!" He underscores the value of making sure a profitable market exists for your work before you invest much time or money into selling your woodworking.

Costing Materials

The primary material in making furniture is dimensional stock. This makes costing materials much easier because numerous resources are available for this stock. And as noted many times in this book, competition breeds lower prices. You can probably find your primary furniture stock through a number of suppliers. You will also be purchasing in larger quantities and earning discounts.

Because you use larger quantities of common stock, you can also better track its cost and use the worksheets included in chapter one and the appendix. You will easily determine the cost of materials for a chair, a table or other furniture you build.

Setting Shop Rates

Making furniture combines a variety of skills and tools. Outdoor furniture can be built from rough lumber with few tools. Queen Anne reproductions will require extensive skills, a variety of tools and quite a bit of craftsmanship. Obviously, the shop rate for making one type of furniture is different from that of the other.

Making outdoor furniture from two-by materials, screws and a brushed-on finish will earn the craftsperson a shop rate of $30 to $40 an hour including overhead. Making Victorian tables and chairs will typically bring the craftsperson a shop rate of $50 to $60 an hour. The tools are more expensive, the market is smaller, and the finished product will last longer.

Estimating Overhead

How much you allow for overhead depends on the number of tools required to produce furniture and cabinetry. Typical tools include a table saw, radial-arm saw, band saw, jointer, drill press, portable drill, router, circular saw, miter saw, sander and planer. Common hand tools include measuring devices, squares, calipers, miter gauges, hand files, rasps, hand planes, scrapers, claw hammer, mallet, pliers and assorted clamps. You may have other tools you use for specific projects, such as a biscuit cutter for making precision biscuit joints.

Ensuring Profit

Furniture can be a profitable venture, depending on the perceived value of your product and how much competition you have. As a guideline, here are the approximate percentages you should expect for expenses and profit from making furniture:

	% OF WHOLESALE	% OF RETAIL
Materials	30	15
Overhead	20	10
Labor	40	20
Profit	10	5
Sales Costs		50
Total	100%	100%

For example, an oak dining chair that will retail for about $500 will typically cost $75 in materials, $50 for shop tools and overhead, about $100 in labor charges, and earn a $25 profit when whole-saled to the furniture store for $250. Again, these are just estimates. Your furniture may require more materials and less labor or less overhead costs. Or you may decide to sell directly to your customers, reducing the sales costs to 30 percent or less.

Selling Value

Why is your furniture more valuable than furniture made by someone else? Your customers probably won't ask you this question directly, but it is always in their minds. Answer it before they ask. Talk about how the customer will benefit from buying furniture you make:

- Their grandchildren will be able to enjoy it.
- Others will admire their choice for many years.
- Their home will feel more comfortable.
- They will enjoy its use every day for many years.

What they are really asking is: Will the value I gain be greater than the value of the money I trade for it? Be proud of your work and tell your customers, verbally or in writing, why their decision to buy your furniture is a smart one.

Outdoor Furniture

Many successful furniture builders have started their trade making outdoor furniture. Why? Because it is popular, requires a smaller investment in tools and time, and can be built with basic woodworking skills. Popular outdoor furniture includes picnic tables, chairs, rockers, tables, lounges and settees, porch swings, benches, planters and barbecues.

As you've discovered, simplicity means competition. You will find many other woodworkers in your area making outdoor furniture. But by studying the local market and talking with home improvement and garden shops, you can determine which products are being overproduced and which will fill a local need.

Shop Rate

Making outdoor furniture also means your shop rate will be lower than with other woodworking products because fewer tools and skills are needed. You can increase your shop rate, however, by developing an efficient production system. Shop rates for making rough outdoor furniture — picnic benches, lounges and planters — are typically $35 to $45 an hour, with the higher rate going to woodworkers with popular designs. Finer outdoor furniture such as unique lounges and settees can earn the woodworker a shop rate of $45 to $55 an hour.

One successful woodworker decided to build and sell Adirondack furniture directly to the public. He lives next to a busy highway, so he opens his garage on weekends and displays completed pieces in the driveway. Adirondack furniture is a rustic style popular during the first half of this century. Its popularity returned in the 1980s, and in some regions it was oversold. However, this style can still be profitably made and sold by woodworkers in many areas of the country.

Benches and Chairs

Indoor furniture such as rustic or pioneer benches and chairs are also good products for furniture makers with less experience or fewer tools. They can earn while they learn. Related items include old-fashioned milk stools, rocking chairs, porch settees and a wide variety of bench and chair designs. Some woodworkers specialize in a single item such as custom workbenches.

The benches and chairs category is so broad that specific pricing is impractical. Woodworkers who produce simple benches and chairs can establish a shop rate similar to that of simple outdoor furniture: $35 to $45 an hour. However, the upper end is higher. Making quality and elaborate benches and chairs can earn a woodworker a shop rate of up to $55 an hour. By specializing in a series of related products, such as dining room chairs or children's rocking chairs, the woodworker can increase efficiency by mass-producing components without sacrificing quality. This makes production more efficient and earns a higher shop rate than if the woodworker made a complete product before starting another.

Tables

Imagine a house without a table. Tables are a valuable component of living, as well as a profitable opportunity for woodworkers to share their skills. Tables come in all sizes and shapes, from simple plant stands to ornate dining tables with leaves. Types of tables include coffee tables, end tables, fern stands, tilt-top tables, washstands, nightstands, drop-leaf tables, parlor tables, telephone stands, breakfast tables, harvest tables, tavern tables, tea tables and worktables. Woods include oak, cherry, maple, walnut, birch, pine, poplar and chestnut.

A *Woodshop News* survey of craft shops reports that occasional tables are the second most popular woodcraft products with their customers.

Shop Rate

Because tables are so necessary, woodworkers who make them can often establish a higher shop rate for their production than for some other furniture requiring the same skills to produce. Table production can earn a shop rate of $45 to $60 an hour. Like other woodworking products, the greater the demand and skills, the higher the shop rate. For example, simple fern stands of softwoods must compete with similar stands sold unassembled at many discount stores. The shop rate for making them will be on the lower end of the scale: about $45 an hour. Making unique oak drop-leaf tables may earn the craftsperson a shop rate of $50 or $55 an hour. The tools required are nearly identical. The difference is simply the value perceived by the customer. If they can buy a "similar" piece at Wal-Mart for $49.95, they will be reluctant to spend three times that for your product.

Chests

Besides function, wooden chests offer artistry and beauty. An oak chest of drawers can add a statement of quality to a room while serving a functional purpose. It can also give the woodworker an opportunity to express his or her craft in a valuable way. Chests include a dresser with mirror, a bureau, an armoire, a hope chest, and a tape or CD cabinet.

Pricing for individual chests can vary from $500 to $1,500 or more for a four-drawer chest. A dresser with mirror is typically priced at up to twice the amount of a chest, depending on the type and price of the mirror. Of course, a pine chest and dresser will be priced at one-third to one-half of these

prices. With experience, some woodworkers price their chests "by the drawer." This doesn't take into account the many variables between chest designs, but it gives them a starting point and simplifies the pricing process for them.

Shop Rate

The shop rate for chests is typically slightly lower than for tables. Many woodworkers establish an hourly shop rate of $40 to $50 for simple chests in softwoods and $50 to $60 for chests from hardwoods or for designs that require advanced skills or tools. Higher shop rates reduce your market but increase the customer's perception of your work's value. This perception is underscored if you develop a unique design that emphasizes your craftsmanship.

Shaker Furniture

Shaker is a popular style of furniture that stresses simple design and quality craftsmanship. It was initiated by the Shakers, a religious communal organization founded in upstate New York near the end of the 18th century. The style continues today in both concept and reproductions. Other regional styles of furniture also illustrate simplicity and functionality. Though they are not true Shaker designs, their construction and their pricing are similar.

The Shakers made more than just furniture. They also made unique baskets, blankets, coffeepots, dust mops, tools and rugs. But they are most famous for their furniture designs: tables, desks, chairs, rockers, settees, benches, stools, chests, cupboards, butter churns, spinning wheels and many other everyday items.

THE WOODWORKER'S GUIDE TO PRICING YOUR WORK

Shop Rate

Because of the popularity of Shaker and other regional styles of furniture, they often get a premium price. In fact, dozens of woodworking shops throughout the East and Midwest specialize in making Shaker-style originals and reproductions. Shop rates for these woodworking shops range from about $45 an hour to over $60 an hour. Typical is $50 an hour. Their shop rate also depends on their distribution system. Shops that sell directly to the public apply some of their normal marketing expenses to their shop rate. A few that sell directly to the public set up their shops in historic towns and shopping areas, opening their shops to the public.

Antique Reproductions

A related category of furniture is antique reproductions. Hundreds of woodworking shops across the United States do nothing but make reproductions of antique furniture. It's big business. That makes it competitive for those who reproduce common antiques and profitable for those who bring unique antiques to the market.

Not everyone can afford period pieces. For example, an original ladder-back Shaker chair can cost $1,500. An Edward Duffield grandfather clock is valued at nearly $10,000. A modern reproduction of an antique will cost a third to a half of the price of the real thing. That's why making and selling antique reproductions has become so popular with woodworkers.

Unfortunately, the term "reproduction" has received a bad name because some buyers associate it with "fake." Manufacturers here and overseas have made exact reproductions of antique furniture and other items without labeling them as such. In fact, some have intentionally sold these reproductions as originals. The difference between a repro-

duction and a fake is the truth. An honest woodworker will mark a reproduction as such.

Producing antique reproductions can offer a number of advantages over other types of woodworking. Antiques are recognized by the public as having more value than products of today. They also understand that reproductions give them the look of an antique without having to pay the higher prices. Reproductions are a compromise. The woodworker benefits from this association.

In addition, the design work is already done. From drawings, photos or actual antiques, you can inexpensively replicate the design. You can also apply modern woodworking techniques and products to overcome some of the inherent design problems of antique furniture.

Shop Rate

The shop rate for making antique reproductions is typically 10 to 20 percent higher than for similar modern designs. That is, a reproduction of a simple antique chest will carry a shop rate of $40 to $50 plus an extra $4 to $8 per hour. Final shop rate will then range from $44 to $58 an hour in this example. As always, many variables exist, including the complexity of the design, the competitive market, distribution methods and tools required to reproduce the antique design.

The best way to learn if antique reproduction is a profitable business for you is to study your market. If you live near a historic community, visit it to analyze what sells and why. Also visit vacation communities in your region. Because many of your antique reproductions will be purchased over the weekend by visitors, check out these towns in your area. (If you live in such a community, all the better.) Visit on the weekend or during the summer and ask people what they're looking for. You may find an untapped market that you can reach with your woodworking skills.

Children's Furniture

Making child-size furniture is an entire market unto itself. In most cases, woodworkers who make children's furniture sell their products directly to the public. In some cases they can find retail outlets that will sell some of their products.

Children's furniture includes beds, youth chairs, training chairs, chests, rocking cradles, standing cradles, cribs, desks, high chairs, ladder-back chairs and rockers.

One successful woodworker built a variety of antique furniture reproductions at half-scale for affluent buyers in New England. Products included rockers, dining tables with chairs, hutches, iceboxes and bedroom furniture. He advertised in regional magazines aimed at this audience and also relied on word-of-mouth advertising.

Makers of children's furniture can establish a shop rate between $40 and $55 an hour. This is a wide range to cover the diverse skills and market for these products. A woodworker making simple desks for children will earn $40 to $45 an hour, while another woodworker designing and making miniature antique replicas may get a shop rate of $55 an hour or more.

Custom Furniture

Some woodworkers specialize in designing and building custom furniture to the individual requirements of the client. In most cases, these craftspeople have extensive skills and experience and have developed a local reputation for their work. Because of these factors, they can typically earn a higher shop rate than most other woodworkers.

Custom-furniture makers sell to individuals, businesses, churches and fraternal organizations. They sometimes work directly for the client, but in most cases they work through a home builder or an interior designer. Obviously, the further they are from the client, the lower the shop rate will be as builders and designers absorb the responsibilities of marketing. It can be nice, however, to have others do the legwork.

Custom-furniture makers build everything from desks to entertainment consoles to unique office furniture. Those who can also design these products can earn more than woodworkers who require a detailed plan from others. Shop rates for custom-furniture makers are on the high side of the spectrum, from $45 to as much as $65 an hour for designers/woodworkers. A select few have earned a reputation that allows them a shop rate of over $75 an hour.

Specialties

Custom-furniture makers in larger cities can specialize in woodworking products such as desks or bookshelves for executives. Others specialize in pews and chairs for churches. In smaller towns, woodworkers may do both production and custom work, varying their shop rate to match the market. Making custom furniture is typically not an entry-level venture. It is for experienced woodworkers who prefer creativity over mass-production. It also requires the development of a reputation and the marketing of your skills. It is as much a lifestyle as it is a craft.

Basics of Pricing Cabinetry

A cabinet is a furniture unit with shelves, drawers or compartments for storing or displaying items. A cabinet can be freestanding — not attached to a wall — or it can be built-in or attached to a wall or other cabinets.

Some cabinetmakers prebuild cabinets to standard dimensions and sell them for installation in kitchens, bathrooms, and other areas of the home. Other cabinetmakers design and build cabinets specifically for an individual home; this is called custom cabinetry. Even so, most "custom" cabinets are built to standard dimensions.

Costing Materials

Making cabinets is similar to making furniture; both use dimensional stock. In fact, cabinets depend on dimensional stock more than furniture does. Because of these factors, material costs are a larger component of the final price of cabinets, but labor is less. In addition, you will find many resources for your materials, allowing comparative shopping and discount pricing.

An old rule of thumb for pricing cabinetry is multiplying the cost of materials by 3.5. This is not very accurate as it doesn't take into account the variation in material pricing, the ease or difficulty of the project, or value pricing. Instead, a cabinetmaker should start with percentages discussed under "Ensuring Profit" and modify them to fit individual skills and situations.

Setting Shop Rates

Cabinetmaking can be a very profitable business, especially for woodworkers who have developed advanced skills and have earned a reputation within their area. While beginning cabinetmakers earn a shop rate of $40 to $50 an hour, experienced cabinetmakers can get a shop rate of $55 to $65 an hour. Part of the value they sell is their name. That is, an experienced cabinetmaker who has designed and built cabinets for a prestigious home or office can get a higher shop rate on future jobs.

Estimating Overhead

A large part of your overhead costs will be the cost of purchasing and maintaining tools. Typical tools

for cabinetmaking include a table saw, radial arm saw, band saw, jointer, drill press, portable drill, router, circular saw, sander and planer. Common hand tools include measuring devices, squares, calipers, miter gauges, hand files, rasps, hand planes, scrapers, claw hammer, mallet, pliers and assorted clamps. You may have other tools you use for specific projects, such as a compound miter saw for cabinet-door frames.

Ensuring Profit

As mentioned earlier, multipliers can't always give you an accurate price for your cabinets. In fact, even percentages aren't completely accurate. But they do offer a starting point from which you can establish your own pricing guidelines and ensure a profit. Here are the typical percentages for cabinetmakers:

	% OF WHOLESALE	% OF RETAIL
Materials	40	20
Overhead	20	10
Labor	30	15
Profit	10	5
Sales Costs	___	50
Total	100%	100%

For example, a set of kitchen cabinets built to retail at $8,000 will have an approximate materials cost of $1,600, an overhead expense of $800, a labor cost of about $1,200 and a profit of $400 to wholesale for $4,000. Many custom cabinetmakers do their own selling, adding another 30 percent to the wholesale price to bring it up to $5,200. Or they will price it at the full retail price of $8,000 and increase their percentages to materials, overhead, labor and profit.

Selling Value

The pricing strategy just illustrated — increasing the direct price from wholesale to retail — requires the cabinetmaker to sell value. The cabinetmaker must show the customer why his or her cabinets are of equal or greater value than competing products. One way to do this is to develop name value, such as "Quality cabinets by J. Smith." This takes more than a stick-on label inside the cabinet door. It takes selling the value of your name through advertising, referrals and marketing, as discussed in chapter five.

Another method of selling value is to include a "free" upgrade into your pricing. The upgrade may be better quality hinges or hardware, a higher quality finish, beveled rather than standard glass — anything that will clearly illustrate that your product is of better quality than that of your competition.

Freestanding Cabinetry

The difference between furniture and freestanding cabinetry is a fine line. In many cases, the terms are interchangeable depending on who is making the unit, a furniture maker or a cabinetmaker. In either case, freestanding cabinetry offers an opportunity for woodworkers to earn a profit from their skills and creativity.

Freestanding cabinetry includes any units that could be installed as a cabinet but aren't. Examples are buffet cabinets, hutches, bookcases, TV and stereo cabinets, entertainment centers, country dry sinks, iceboxes, pie safes, etc. Individual units are typically priced at between $500 and $2,500 each. Woodworkers who want to survive will not compete with the $79.95 entertainment centers available at discount stores. In fact, do whatever you can to make them not look like these units.

Shop Rate

Simple freestanding cabinetry such as bookcases and entertainment centers requires fewer skills and tools, so woodworkers typically earn a shop rate of $45 to $50 an hour. Units that offer a unique design

may earn a higher shop rate. Freestanding cabinets that require more skills and tools — or are perceived to be more valuable — can earn a shop rate of $55 or more an hour. Examples are hutches and buffets, especially those designed as replicas of period furniture. You can also add value by installing interior lighting, upgrading glass to beveled or leaded, or gold-leafing an interior surface.

One successful woodworker developed a short buffet table that sold well while giving her a profitable shop rate. She then designed and sold matching units to these same customers, increasing total sales with little investment in marketing. Rather than find new customers she simply resold her existing customers. She has since moved on to more artistic woodworking, funded by her success as a freestanding-cabinet maker.

Kitchen Cabinetry

For many homeowners, the kitchen is the most important room of the house. As any real estate agent will tell you, a beautiful kitchen can sell an otherwise commonplace house. And when remodeling, homeowners often choose the kitchen as the first room to be enhanced. That's why many successful woodworkers specialize in making and installing kitchen cabinets.

Most kitchen cabinets are a standard height and width. The primary differences are in the wood selected and the door design. Because many of the designs and components are similar, a cabinetmaker can set up a shop that will increase efficiency and reduce waste. Jigs can be made for drilling holes for shelf pegs, for routing doors and for installing hinges, reducing the time required to complete these necessary tasks.

New kitchen cabinets are a major investment for the homeowner of $4,000 to $15,000 or more. The woodworker who specializes in kitchen cabinets must make sure that the deposit at least covers the cost of materials. Most experienced woodworkers use standard remodeling contracts available from large stationery stores to establish a binding contract with the customer. While some risk exists of not getting paid in full, a prudent cabinetmaker can minimize the risk.

An advantage to making kitchen cabinets is that the cost of marketing is a smaller percentage of the total. Many successful kitchen-cabinet makers spend no more than 25 percent of their income on marketing. Those who have developed a strong reputation and depend on repeat and referral customers may spend as little as 5 percent of sales on marketing, primarily for an ad in the telephone book.

Shop Rate

The typical shop rate for a kitchen-cabinet maker is $40 to $50 an hour. Some part-timers charge less to get their business started, and experienced cabinetmakers may get more, but most fall within this range.

Those who apply multipliers to price their work usually use 3.5 or 4. That is, a kitchen-cabinet job requiring $2,000 in materials will be priced at $7,000 to $8,000. Many experienced woodworkers, however, recommend that detailed pricing sheets be used rather than multipliers. Multipliers don't take into account difficult installations or related services such as installing countertops and splashes. Completing a pricing sheet will take only a few minutes more and can save you hundreds of dollars.

Square-Footage Pricing

One successful kitchen-cabinet maker found that measuring the square footage of cabinets offered the most accurate pricing. He started using multipliers, then went to shop rates, to eventually come up with square-foot prices that kept pricing both competitive and profitable.

You may actually have two shop rates: one for cabinet design and construction, and a lower rate for installation. Installation rates are typically about two-thirds of the full rate. That is, a cabinetmaker with a construction shop rate of $50 an hour may charge only $35 an hour for installation. Tools and skills used during installation are less than those used to make the cabinets. Or the installation time may be factored into a single construction and installation rate. Remember that if you physically install cabinets in a dwelling, you may be required to obtain a contractor's license. Talk with your state contractor's board about requirements and testing.

Bath Cabinetry

Making and installing cabinets in bathrooms is simpler than for kitchens. That's why many cabinetmakers prefer bath cabinets. It also gives them a chance to sell related items like towel racks, mirrored cabinets and over-tank cabinets that they can produce in quantity during slower times.

Bath-cabinet makers typically charge a shop rate that is approximately the same as for kitchen cabinets: $45 to $55 an hour. The exception is where competition from stock cabinets lowers the price you can get for your units. Of course, as suggested throughout this book, your response to low prices should be high value. Find a way to make your woodworking products visibly different and of higher value than those of your competitors.

Custom Cabinetry

As you develop experience and skills in cabinetmaking, you will be asked to design and make distinctive cabinets for customers. Pricing these unique products may seem a formidable task. Yet they are just as easy to price as any other woodworking product. The advantage to custom cabinetry is that, in many cases, you have no competition for the job. You can ask for a higher shop rate that reflects your enhanced skills and still get the job.

Custom cabinetry requires more skills and experience than making stock or near-stock cabinets. Your shop rate should reflect this. Some experienced cabinetmakers establish a rate for custom cabinets at $50 to $55 an hour or more. Those who primarily make stock cabinets but are sometimes called on to produce custom units will increase their standard shop rate by 10 to 20 percent for such jobs. That is, a cabinetmaker who typically gets $50 an hour for his cabinets may charge $55 to $60 an hour for designing and making custom cabinets. Whether you select a "custom surcharge" of 10 percent or 20 percent depends on the complexity of the job, the competition and the needs of the customer. If you know the customer will be difficult to work with and probably ask for changes, charge the higher percentage.

Increasing Profits *without* Reducing Quality

Now that your small woodworking venture is profitable, many ways exist in which you can make it even more so. You don't have to reduce the quality of your work or your product. In fact, you'll find that quality will probably improve as you build and sell more woodworking products, learning from each one. Many successful woodworkers have increased profits without reducing quality. So can you. This chapter will show you how.

Jim Streeter of J.M. Streeter Woodworking offers this advice to beginners: "Go back to school and learn about business before you attempt to start one." Many craftspeople who manage their own businesses either fail within the first two years or struggle along for many years until they learn the basics of business — the hard way. Jim suggests, as other professional woodworkers do, that you must learn about profit as well as about wood. Take small-business courses offered by local colleges, business development centers and other groups. It will give you the tools you need to make money and do what you love.

Almost Painless Record Keeping

Most woodworkers and craftspeople dislike keeping records, even though they understand the necessity. To them, profit is whatever is left in the wallet at the end of the month. Estimated taxes are always underestimated. A budget is what they'll set up next year.

Your record-keeping system doesn't have to be complex to set up or painful to use. Your woodworking venture has only a couple of items that must be recorded: how much you receive and how much you spend. Beyond that you can make your job easier by keeping more detailed records, but they aren't necessary.

This chapter offers numerous easy-to-use record-keeping forms. In addition, chapter six covers computer software, including those that make record keeping easier.

Figure 5-1 illustrates a Cash Receipts Journal for recording money you receive. Figure 5-2 is a Cash Disbursements Journal for recording money you spend. Blank forms in the appendix of this book can be customized and copied for your woodworking business.

If you prefer, a stationery store or large discount store will have bound books of lined paper with two columns (a journal) for less than $5 each. Label the first column "Income" and the second "Expenses." On each line, write the date, from whom you received money or to whom you paid money, and the amount in one of the two columns. At the end of each page write "Balance Forward," total the columns, and copy the "Balances" to the first line of the next page. Then you can determine what your current income and expenses are at any time. Subtract expenses from income and you know what your profit (or loss) is.

Some woodworkers will use the front of their journal for recording their checkbook entries, and the pages in the back for keeping track of cash payments. You will use checks for most of what you buy, but sometimes you don't want to write a check for two pounds of 6d nails or a packet of sandpaper, and so you pay cash. Keep the receipt. Keep track of these small cash payments, called *petty cash*. Once a month or whenever they total more than about $50, write a check to yourself for the total of all these business receipts. As your hobby becomes a business it becomes more important to separate your personal money from that of your business.

Tracking Jobs and Time
How can you keep track of jobs and your time? The simplest way is to write everything down in one location: a wall calendar, a Day-Timer (www.daytimer.com, 800-457-5702) or Planner

Creative Woodcraft Inc.

123 Main Street, Yourtown USA 12345

Cash Receipts Journal

PERIOD ENDING: March 31, 2005

Date	Check Number	Account Number	Amount	Name
March 3	2745	234	478.50	Bill Johnson (down payment on bathroom cabinets)
March 7	965	229	2534.00	Mary Smith (final payment on kitchen cabinets)
March 19	543	233	196.00	Nancy Miller (additional cabinets)
March 24	1023	256	589.00	John Ramos (on account)
March 30	789	239	525.00	Wes Loggan (down payment on cabinets for office)

Figure 5-1. Keep a Cash Receipts Journal for recording cash and checks received. A blank form that you can reproduce and use is included in the appendix.

Creative Woodcraft Inc.

Cash Disbursements Journal

123 Main Street, Yourtown USA 12345

PERIOD ENDING: March 31, 2005

Date	Check Number	Account Number	Amount	Name
March 3	1234	489	363.00	Johnson Building Materials (February materials and supplies)
March 4	1235	453	78.22	PacBell (telephone bill)
March 7	1236	432	24.33	UPS (shipping charges)
March 9	1237	456	58.50	PGE (utilities)
March 13	1238	421	74.32	Petty Cash (replentish)
March 20	1239	454	891.40	Bart's Tools (shop tools)
March 24	1240	463	218.00	Smith River Lumber (materials)
March 31	1241	444	1500.00	Capital Draw (salary)

Figure 5-2. A Cash Disbursements Journal records payments by cash or check. A blank form that you can reproduce and use is included in the appendix.

Pads (www.plannerpads.com, 800-315-7526), or a bound record book from the same source as your ledger. Everything is in one place. It may be disorganized, but it's there. A better method is to keep separate records of each job you're doing, either in file folders or in a three-ring binder. Some woodworkers do both; they have a job file and a calendar to write nonjob notes.

To make the task of keeping time records easier, the appendix of this book includes a number of useful forms that you can copy and customize.

Estimating Your Breakeven Point

A simple calculation called the breakeven point can help you make your woodworking venture more profitable. The breakeven point is the point at which income equals expenses. For example, if you sell dollhouses at $100 each and you need $1,000 each month to cover expenses and wages for your part-time venture, your breakeven point is 10 units. If you sell 18 units that month, you've made a healthy profit. If you sell only eight units, you've lost money.

Calculate Fixed and Variable Costs

To estimate your breakeven point, you need to add up all your fixed costs (wages, rent, equipment, etc.) and variable costs (materials, etc.). A fixed cost is one that goes on whether you sell anything or not. A variable cost changes as you make and sell products. Adding these two costs together tells you how much you need to make each month. Divide this by the amount you will receive for a typical product. If you make many woodworking products, you may have a number of breakeven points, depending on which products you sell. In the above example, you may need to sell 18 small doll-houses or nine large ones to break even each month. If you usually sell four small dollhouses for every large unit, you need to sell about 12 small units and three large units each month.

Knowing your woodworking business's breakeven point can help you decide whether to concentrate more on marketing or on production that month. It can help you stay profitable.

Spreadsheet Programs

If you have a computer that you can use for your business records, you should invest in a spreadsheet program, such as Microsoft Excel. You can purchase a basic spreadsheet program that will let you enter horizontal rows or lines of job expense names (Labor, Materials, etc.) and vertical columns of numbers ($428.52, etc.) for about $100. Most important, you can then tell the program to total any or all of the columns or rows and it will do so in less than a second. If you update a number, it automatically recalculates the total for you.

Most spreadsheet programs can follow sets of instructions you write, called macros, to do special calculations automatically. You could, for example, write a macro that will select all the invoices over 60 days old and total them. Most will also produce fancy graphs and pie charts that impress lenders and other financial types.

Managing Cash Flow

One of the biggest complaints heard from business owners is that money doesn't come in as fast as it must go out. Even though the business has more sales dollars than expense dollars, making those sales dollars arrive on time can be a big headache. Your woodworking enterprise will be no exception.

How do large businesses tackle this headache? They manage their cash flow. They keep track of not only sales, but when sales will turn into

Creative Woodcraft Inc.

123 Main Street, Yourtown USA 12345

Cash Flow Forecast

DATE:

FOR TIME PERIOD: February, 2005

APPROVED BY:

PREPARED BY:

	Date:		Date:		Date:	
	ESTIMATE	ACTUAL	ESTIMATE	ACTUAL	ESTIMATE	ACTUAL
Opening Balance	$3,000.00	$3,211.45				
Collections From Trade	$4,150.00	$3,930.00				
Misc. Cash Receipts						
TOTAL CASH AVAILABLE	$7,150.00	$7,141.45				
DISBURSEMENTS						
Payroll	$3,740.00	$3,225.00				
Trade Payables						
Other		$175.00				
Capital Expenses	$1,600.00	$1,600.00				
Income Tax	$500.00	$496.50				
Bank Loan Payment	250	$250.00				
TOTAL DISBURSEMENTS	$6,090.00	$5,746.50				
FOR INTERNAL USE ONLY						
Ending Balance	$1,060.00	$1,394.95				
Less Minimum Balance	$2,000.00	$2,000.00				
CASH AVAILABLE	($940.00)	($605.05)				

Figure 5-3. A Cash Flow Forecast helps you pay your bills on time and sleep better at night. A blank form that you can reproduce and use is included in the appendix.

income. That is, if you've sold 12 lamps to a wholesaler at $110 each, you have a sale of $1,320, but maybe no income for 30, 60, or 90 days or more. What do you do in the meantime to buy needed materials, make machinery repairs and pay for shipping costs?

Projecting Income

One option is to require payments on specific dates, with a late fee for missing those dates. That way you can project when you will get income and make plans accordingly. You will then write those expected payments on a cash flow projection or forecast (Figure 5-3). You will include other time payments to get a clearer picture of when sales dollars will become income dollars.

Another option for improving cash flow is to set a firm credit policy and stick to it. Your policy may be any of the following:

• Cash or local check on delivery
• Cash, check or credit card
• Net 30 days or 2/10 net 30

Many businesses offer the terms 2/10 (two-off-ten) net 30. That means the customer gets a 2 percent discount for payment within 10 days, but the net invoice amount is due and payable within 30 days.

Credit Card Sales

Offering to allow payment by credit card will definitely increase your sales to retail customers. Many people are more inclined to buy if they can put it on their Visa, MasterCard or Discover card. How can you help them buy? Chances are, until your woodworking business grows, you will not be able to get your bank to set you up as a credit card merchant. Besides, doing so can be expensive; you need specific equipment (cost: about $500) and you must pay a fee (2 to 4 percent) on each transaction. You may be able to lease the equipment, but costs per transaction are still high if you don't sell a minimum amount on charge cards.

An alternative: Some banks will allow you to take transactions on charge cards without being a card merchant. They give you the required forms and instructions, which you fill out for the customer and return to the bank. The bank then processes the transaction for you. You will be charged an additional transaction fee, but it can save you the expenses of purchasing transaction equipment you will rarely use. This option allows you to offer charge cards as a payment option — and improve your cash flow — without a major investment. If this sounds right for you, talk with your banker or other bankers in your area.

In any case, beware of offers from firms that will get you credit merchant status for an up-front fee. Some are reputable, but too many are not. In some cases, the fees are exorbitant or the firms don't do what they promise. A small business cannot afford to make $1,000 mistakes very often. Play it safe and work with your bank or a trusted trade association if you want to offer payment by credit card.

Staying Out of Business Traps

The biggest business trap that woodworkers and other craftspeople get into is the credit game. Maybe that new planer isn't a necessity for making your product. In fact, buying and using it will cost more than having your stock planed for you. Sure, it would look nice in your shop — and the salesperson says you can have it for just $4.92 a day! The equipment needs shop space, now at a premium. You should also upgrade your ventilation system to handle the additional dust. The list goes on. What was just $4.92 a day is now cutting deeply into your profits, as well as the time available to make those profits.

Handling Credit

How can you stay out of the credit trap? By not using credit. That's difficult to do in this world of invoices and "put it on my account." But that's exactly what many small woodworking shops insist on: no credit. They say, "If I can't pay cash for it, I don't need it." This may sound extreme, but many successful woodworkers have managed their businesses for years with this policy.

Another option is to set a more realistic credit policy: 30 days. That is, woodworkers pick up materials from their suppliers on credit, but they pay the bill in full at the end of each month. No carryover. No revolving credit. And these craftspeople offer the same terms to their customers: payment in full within 30 days. Of course, this credit policy may limit your sales. But many woodworkers feel it is the only way to stay out of the credit trap.

Tax Problems

Another trap faced by businesses of all sizes is paying too much in taxes. Once you attempt to make a profit with your woodworking tools and skills, the value of those tools is a legitimate expense that you can deduct from your income. Of course, some people go overboard and decide to deduct their living room furniture because "a customer once sat on it." Probably not legal! However, the shop tools you've collected over the years can be valued, then declared as a legitimate expense. So can the cost of your shop. Make sure you declare these expenses on your federal and state income taxes. Get — and read — the IRS publications suggested in chapter one.

Developing Your Business

Get a Business Phone

Many of the successful woodworkers interviewed for this book said that a separate business telephone is a necessity, especially if you have teenagers or other excessive phone users in the family. You will also need an answering system, particularly if your business is a part-time venture. You could be losing half of your business by not having a professional and efficient phone system. The cost of a business line has decreased over the last few years because of the competition among telephone companies.

If you will be answering with a business name rather than a personal name, you need a business phone line. If your name is Bob Jones and your firm is Bob Jones Woodworking, you can answer "Bob Jones" and not confuse your prospects and clients. But if you're Quality Woodworking and you answer "Bob Jones," some callers may think they have the wrong number.

If you will also be using dial-up Internet (chapter six), consider a second line if you plan to be on more than 20 minutes a day during normal business hours. You could miss customer calls while you "surf the net."

Answering Systems

Not long ago, an answering system was an annoying and misused tape recorder that attempted to drive off the people that called you. Today's answering system is much more accepted, especially in business. It's also easier to buy and use.

Tape answering machines will use either mini- or standard-size audiotapes to record an outgoing and any incoming messages. The good ones have a separate tape for each. The better ones don't have time limits for incoming messages. The best ones have features that allow you to hear your messages from any other telephone, can let you know if you have any messages at all, and will allow you to easily change your messages from a remote location.

Digital answering machines use computer chips to record outgoing messages and, in some cases, incoming calls. The sound quality is often better, but the length of the message may be limited. However, advances in digital-sound technology will make next year's models even more useful. Be certain that the system you purchase announces the date and time of the call on the incoming message so you know when the call came in.

Your local telephone company may offer voice mail service to answer your phone for you in your absence or while you are on the phone. This means your customers won't get a busy signal and you won't miss their calls. Other advantages to voice mail are that it works even during a power failure, unlike a conventional answering machine, and you purchase no equipment. Check with your phone company for particulars on signing up for voice mail service.

Unfortunately, many businesses misuse their answering system by putting cryptic announcements and background music on the system that confuse or intimidate callers. An effective message should be something like:

"Hello, this is Quality Woodworking's answering system. Your call is important to us. Please leave your name and telephone number after the beep and someone will get back to you as soon as possible. Or if you'd prefer, please call again later. Thank you."

Remember: If you want your business to be successful, it must sound successful.

Free Business Advice

As your woodworking business grows you will have numerous questions about keeping records, paying taxes, finding new markets, extending credit, reducing losses and locating sources for financing new equipment.

Small Business Development Centers

Small Business Development Centers (SBDCs) are regional centers funded by the U.S. Small Business Administration (SBA) and managed in conjunction with regional colleges. An SBDC offers free and confidential counseling for small-business owners and managers, new businesses, home-based businesses and people with business ideas, including retail, service, wholesale, manufacturing and farm businesses. They sponsor seminars on various business topics, assist in developing business and marketing plans, inform entrepreneurs of employer requirements and teach cash flow budgeting and management. SBDCs also gather information sources, assist in locating business resources and make referrals.

Call your local SBA office or college campus to determine if a Small Business Development Center is near you, and if so, what services they will provide as you build your woodworking business. You can find the SBA on the Internet at www.sba.gov.

SCORE

The Service Corps of Retired Executives (SCORE; 409 Third Street, SW, 6th Floor, Washington, DC, 20024; 800-634-0245; www.score.org) is a national nonprofit association with the goal of helping small businesses. SCORE members include retired men and women — as well as those who are still active in their own businesses — who donate their time and experience to counsel individuals regarding small business. SCORE is sponsored by the U.S. Small Business Administration, and the local office is usually in or near that of the local SBA office.

A SCORE counselor can help you write your business plan at no charge. To take advantage of the counseling services of a SCORE counselor, complete a SCORE Request for Counseling worksheet and return it to the local office in person or by mail. The interview will be in person at a mutually agreed on time. The questionnaire will ask: the type of business; whether you're starting, buying or currently operating the business; how much experience you have in this business; how much accounting knowledge you have; and the type of question you have.

SCORE counselors are typically highly experienced business people; some may have direct experience in the woodworking and crafts businesses. You are not charged for their time and assistance, nor are you required to follow their advice. But the more counselors you have, the greater the opportunity for success as a professional woodworker.

How to Pay Taxes

Even a part-time business is required to pay income taxes on profits. Actually, you may play two roles in managing taxes. In one role, you're a debtor; in the other, an agent or tax collector. As a debtor, you're liable for various taxes and you pay them as part of your business obligations. For example, each year you owe federal income taxes that you pay out of the earnings of your business. You may also pay state income taxes on your woodworking profits.

As an agent, you may collect taxes and pass the funds on to a government agency. If your state requires retail sales tax on your woodworking products, you will collect it from your customers. Of course, if you sell your woodworking only on a wholesale basis, you won't have to worry about collecting and passing along sales tax. If you have employees, you deduct federal income and social security insurance (FICA) taxes, and in some states, state income taxes from the wages of your employees.

Necessary Tax Forms

If you are a proprietor, you pay your income tax in the same way as any other individual citizen: Your income, expenses, and profit or loss are calculated on Schedule C, which is filed with your annual Form 1040. Partnerships and corporations use other tax forms. Self-employment tax – social security insurance for the self-employed – is reported on your Form 1040 using Schedule SE.

Individual proprietors and partners are required by law to put the federal income tax and self-employment tax liability on a pay-as-you-go basis. That is, you file a declaration of estimated tax using Form 1040-ES on or before April 15, then make payments on April 15, June 15, September 15 and January 15.

To find out more about your tax obligations, contact your regional IRS office (or call 800-829-3676; www.irs.gov) for the following publications:

- Employer's Tax Guide (Publication 15 Circular E)
- Your Federal Income Tax (Publication 17)
- Tax Guide for Small Business (Publication 334)
- Tax Withholding and Estimated Tax (Publication 505)
- Self-Employment Tax (Publication 533)
- Retirement Plans for Small Business (Publication 560)
- Starting a Business and Keeping Records (Publication 583)
- Business Use of Your Home (Publication 587)
- Guide to Free Tax Services (Publication 910)

Effective Craft Show Sales Techniques

The largest sales opportunity for woodworkers is often craft shows and outdoor art festivals. Depending on your specialty, you may sell all or most — or none — of your woodworking projects at craft shows and fairs. Selling through craft fairs requires that you spend as much as half of your time preparing for or attending shows. The majority of retail craft shows estimate an average sale of between $35 and $75, depending on size and publicity.

The cost of a booth at a craft show, fair or festival ranges from $25 to as much as $300 per booth for a weekend. Regional and national show fees are higher and may include a percentage of your sales.

Some show managers will rent you a booth for one day if you wish. If you rent the booth for a two-day weekend, your agreement will probably require that you have someone at the show for all show hours unless another arrangement is made. Most shows are open from about 10 a.m. to 5 p.m., depending on the type of show, the theme of the show (holiday, event, year-round, etc.) and local customs. Many shows don't open on Sunday until after 12 p.m. to allow for church attendance.

As you exhibit at craft shows and keep good sales records you will soon determine how many sales you can expect per thousand people who attend. You may find that you sell 2.1 whirligigs, for example, for every 1,000 attendees. Or it may be 4.7 wooden toys per 1,000. With this ratio you can better determine whether a specific craft show will be worth your time and effort. By estimating costs to attend the show, calculating the value of your time, and dividing that amount by projected sales, you can estimate the profitability of a specific show. Of course, much depends on your location at the show, the show hours, how many of your competitors are there, the weather and many other factors beyond your control.

Besides retail craft shows and fairs, you can choose to sell your woodworking products at festivals, mall shows and exhibits.

Booth Design

Before designing your booth, visit craft shows where you expect to exhibit. Find the information booth and get an exhibitor's package with information on booth size, requirements and limitations. Standard booth size is 8' or 10' wide by 10' deep. Plan your booth so that it can be easily modified for various widths and depths without reducing its effectiveness.

As you visit potential craft shows, look at your competitors' booths. How do they encourage people to stop? Is their booth open to invite people to step in, or is it closed to allow more room to store stock? What booth, in your opinion, has the most effective design? Which one has the most people stopping and buying? How do they get people to stop? Does it use banners or large signs or sample crafts or display tables or what? Are prices clearly marked, or do customers have to ask for prices? Apply your creative skills to improve on the best ideas from each show. Design your booth so that new ideas can easily be incorporated into its design without major changes.

Plan your booth so that you are not looking straight at people as they come in to your booth. Even turning your chair sideways in a corner makes the situation less confrontational. Better: Have a woodworking item in your hands, preferably something that encourages people to ask you a question.

Remember to dress the part. That is, if you're selling country wood crafts, dress up like a country craftsmaker. If you make and sell Shaker furniture or reproductions, wear clothing that looks like it comes from that period. It may be just a shirt or shawl or a hat. Even your wearing a shop apron helps customers feel like they are buying from an artisan.

Develop a Mailing List

Depending on your woodworking products, you may want to encourage people who attend craft shows to sign up for your mailing list. In fact, if you sell higher-priced woodworking products, you may find that most of your sales will come from customers who are introduced to you at the shows but don't buy until a relationship is built through direct mail and even telephone contacts. Craft shows become opportunities to show your product and begin the selling process. Sales will be finalized at the customer's home or at your showroom or shop.

To develop a mailing list, leave a sign-up sheet in your booth for a free newsletter or brochure. Some woodworkers offer seasonal discounts to customers on their mailing list. Others send quarterly letters to their mailing list telling customers about shows they will be attending and, if available, offering discount or complimentary tickets to the show.

Know Your Market

Craft shows will also help you determine what doesn't sell. That is, you may want to sell toy chests at craft shows but see that, at shows in your region, toy chests don't sell well enough to cover show expenses. You can consider developing a more novel way of selling them at shows — or you can decide to sell them another way. As you walk the shows, keep a notebook of your observations. Also talk with both exhibitors and attendees to find out what works and what doesn't. You may learn from the trials of experienced craft show exhibitors without having to pay for their mistakes. You'll get a free education that can save you hundreds of dollars and many hours of frustration.

Nancy Bartow, owner of Scholfield Valley Wood Products, makes a variety of wood craft gift items and sells them at art and craft fairs throughout the Pacific Northwest. All her items are under $50 each, and most are priced between $15 and $25 each. She prices her work based on time and materials as well as a comparison with the competition. "We've added and dropped many items over the years because we could not competitively sell them and still make money." She knows her customers well, spending many weekends in her booth talking with craft show buyers.

Resources

If your woodworking sales depend on craft shows, consider subscribing to *The Crafts Report* (100 Rogers Road, Wilmington, DE 19801; 800-777-7098; www.craftsreport.com). It's an excellent publication for those in the business of making and selling crafts. It includes information on shops and galleries looking for crafts, as well as on upcoming craft shows. In addition, the American Craft Council sponsors craft marketing events each year in major cities (72 Spring Street, New York, NY 10012; 800-836-3470; www.craftcouncil.org). These events are about 75 percent wholesale and 25 percent retail. *The Crafts Report* estimates that craft sales add about $350 million a year to the national economy.

Selling at Flea Markets

So-called flea markets can be lucrative sales opportunities for woodworkers. On any given weekend thousands of flea markets are in progress across the nation. Some specialize, but most offer everything from homegrown herbs to handmade pot holders. Here are some ideas on how you can improve your sales through flea markets.

Choosing Your Market and Your Site

First, select a flea market that draws a consistently large crowd, but not so large that the crowd is difficult to manage; promoters may be advertising the flea market widely.

Second, make sure it has a good mix of vendors, and if possible, select a site near vendors of similar products. Don't worry about competition; let them worry about you. Make a good and needed product, price it fairly and sell its value, and you won't have any competition.

Third, be consistent. A flea market attendee may see your booth many times before buying from you. So, as long as it is profitable, have a booth at the flea market every week. If possible, set up your booth at the same site every time; if you can't, make sure your booth is recognizable from a distance with a large sign or unique decoration.

Fourth, make sure that your booth is attractive and encourages buyers to stop and look. Use your creative skills to make a handsome booth. Look at the booths of other vendors and select the best elements from many to incorporate into your design. Of course, also make sure that it is a booth that can be set up in less than an hour and easily stored during the off-season.

Fifth, have something for everyone. If you sell large woodworking products, have a few small items to sell, or even to give away. You can offer smaller versions of your primary wood crafts or related wood products. If possible, offer items starting at just a few dollars for those who feel like they want something you've made, even though they can't afford your primary product. Remember that most people who come to a flea market are just browsing and that you must have some lower-priced products for them to take home.

Finally, have fun. Talk with prospective customers. Use the opportunity to do market research and pricing research and to understand what buyers are looking for.

Specifications

Before you select a flea market, ask the promoter how many square feet of floor space you will get, the dimensions of the space, where the space will be located, what tables or covers the promoter will furnish, what other merchants will be located next to and across from your booth, where the primary traffic pattern is and the hours of the show.

Developing New Sales Channels

Thus far, this book has primarily discussed selling your own woodworking projects. Of course, many other ways exist to sell what you make. Most woodworkers start by selling their own work, so they learn directly from the customer what sells and what doesn't. They develop invaluable knowledge of their market and their craft. Then, because of time limits or preferences, they often sell their products to retailers, who then sell to the general public.

The largest retail market for smaller woodworking products — decorative lamps, candlesticks, wooden boxes, whirligigs and the like — is gift shops and craft shops. Nearly 70,000 gift shops are located in the United States and another 8,000 in Canada. Over 3,000 arts and crafts shops are located in the United States and about 500 in Canada. Together they make up a tremendous opportunity to sell smaller woodworking products with a retail price under $150. Wood products must be smaller because they require shipment, an expense that can take much of the profit of a larger, lower-priced item.

Contacting Craft Shops

A survey of craft shops conducted by *Woodshop News* reports that 91 percent of them will purchase directly from a woodworker who contacts them; 44 percent of them prefer a letter; 30 percent prefer to talk with the craftsperson by phone; and 24 percent accept unannounced visits, as long as it's not at a normally busy time.

A proven way to sell to gift and craft shops is to contact them directly. You'll find their names and addresses in telephone book yellow pages. You can also purchase a mailing list of shops in your state or region. The lists are typically typed labels that you can affix to your brochure or sales package. Mailing lists are available through list brokers and mailing services (see metropolitan phone books) for about $0.12 a name in quantity.

Do a little market research for yourself. Make sure that the craft and gift shops you approach purchase items similar to what you make and in the price range you work in. That is, don't try to sell $1,500 hand-carved exotic bowls to a country wood craft store. To them you would sell pine products made with a band saw and finished with a stencil. How can you learn what a shop prefers to sell? Call them.

Wholesale Craft Shows

Some woodworkers prefer to show their products at wholesale craft shows and sell directly to retailers. The purpose of the show is to give you an opportunity to present your products to as many retailers as possible and to take advance orders. According to the *Woodshop News* craft survey, 81 percent of the craft retailers interviewed go to these shows. Over one-half of all their purchases are made at wholesale shows. This is, obviously, an excellent way for you to meet buyers.

Other Retail Opportunities

If you make larger woodworking items such as furniture or cabinets, furniture stores will offer your best retail sales opportunity. More than 45,000 retail furniture stores are located in the United States and over 5,000 in Canada. Again, list brokers can give you specific names and addresses. Or you can sell through some of the more than 2,500 furniture wholesalers, but be ready for mass production on a small profit margin.

If you make unique works of art with high price tags — exotic turned bowls, hand-carved murals, etc. — offer your work to art galleries and dealers. About 24,000 galleries are located in the United States and another 3,200 in Canada. You'll command a higher price for unique wood products, but

you'll sell fewer.

Antique reproductions and Shaker furniture often sell best at antique stores. More than 35,000 antique dealers are located in the United States and about 2,500 in Canada. Mailing-list brokers can give you a list of them by state, by region and even by specialty: originals, reproductions, furniture-only, etc.

Some woodworking products require creativity in selling as well as making. For example, hand-carved birds can be sold in art galleries, gift shops, museum shops and even upscale nurseries. Clocks can be sold to restaurant supply wholesalers who sell them to restaurants that are building or remodeling, or to large corporations by etching their name into the face glass or into the case.

Pricing Guidelines

A gallery owner told me that some craftspeople are upset when they hear that the gallery will sell the woodworking product for twice what the shop pays for it. For example, a wall plaque for which the woodworker gets $500 is tagged with a retail price of $1,000. Why does the gallery get so much? She explains that, of the retail price, 50 percent goes to the woodworker, about 20 percent goes for overhead to run the shop, and another 20 percent is for labor to staff the shop. That leaves a 10 percent profit before taxes. If the shop owner must give a 10 percent discount to a good customer or put the item on sale, the profit is gone.

As a guideline, expect to sell your woodworking products to retailers at about 50 percent of the retail price. That is, they will typically pay about $150 wholesale for a clock they expect to sell retail at $295. Set your wholesale prices accordingly. If you determine that the clock's cost is $180, you may want to set a wholesale price of $200 and suggest the retail price of $395. Pricing that doubles at each level (manufacturer, wholesaler, retailer) is called keystone pricing.

Creative Woodcraft Inc.

123 Main Street, Yourtown USA 12345

CREDIT APPLICATION

DATE: March 1, 2005

BUSINESS INFORMATION

NAME OF BUSINESS   Gail's Gifts

LEGAL (IF DIFFERENT)   Gail Johnson Enterprises

ADDRESS   456 Main St.

CITY   Yourtown

STATE   AN   ZIP   12345   PHONE   555-1234

DESCRIPTION OF BUSINESS

NO. OF EMPLOYEES	CREDIT REQUESTED	TYPE OF BUSINESS
1	1000	Gift Ship

IN BUSINESS SINCE   1989

BUSINESS STRUCTURE

[ ] CORPORATION   [ ] PARTNERSHIP   [✓] PROPRIETORSHIP

[ ] DIVISION/SUBSIDIARY   NAME OF PARENT COMPANY _____

HOW LONG IN BUSINESS _____

COMPANY PRINCIPALS RESPONSIBLE FOR BUSINESS TRANSACTIONS

NAME:	TITLE:	ADDRESS:	PHONE:
Gail Johnson	Owner	987 Broadway	555-4321
NAME:	TITLE:	ADDRESS:	PHONE:
NAME:	TITLE:	ADDRESS:	PHONE:

BANK REFERENCES

NAME OF BANK   Yourtown Bank

BRANCH   Downtown

CHECKING ACCOUNT NO.   1234567890

NAME TO CONTACT   Jack Jones

ADDRESS   567 Main St., Yourtown

TELEPHONE NUMBER   555-9876

TRADE REFERENCES

FIRM NAME	CONTACT NAME	TELEPHONE NUMBER	ACCOUNT OPEN SINCE
Jeff's Craftw	Jeff Miller	555-2222	1991
Yourtown Woodcraft	Mike Best	555-8888	1989
Jane's Wholesale Crafts	Jane Taylor	555-3456	1990

CONFIRMATION OF INFORMATION ACCURACY AND RELEASE OF AUTHORITY TO VERIFY

I hereby certify that the information in this credit application is correct. The information included in this credit application is for use by he above firm in determining the amount and conditions of credit to be extended. I understand that this firm may also utilize the other sources of credit which it considers necessary in making this determination. Further I hereby authorize the bank and trade references listed in this credit application to release the information necessary to assist this firm in establishing a line of credit.

_____   _____   March 1, 2005
SIGNATURE   TITLE   DATE

POLICY STATEMENT: INITIAL ORDER FROM NEW ACCOUNTS WILL NOT BE PROCESSED UNLESS ACCOMPANIED BY THE ABOVE REQUESTED INFORMATION.
TERMS: NET 30 DAYS FROM DATE OF INVOICE UNLESS OTHERWISE STATED.

Figure 5-4. Here is a typical Credit Application. A blank form that you can reproduce and use is included in the appendix.

Credit Terms

Should you offer terms to retail stores? Much depends on whether your business has sufficient funds to cover the problems that credit can give you. Offering credit terms — a 30-, 60- or 90-day payment plan — instead of cash on delivery can increase your sales, but it can also increase your headaches. Most businesses believe — and profit from — the philosophy of increasing profits through managed credit. That is, as long as you carefully manage credit and to whom you give it you will come out ahead. If you want to keep your woodworking venture small and feel you have sufficient customers to do so, then terms can be cash with order or cash on delivery. But if you're trying to build a part-time business where others have gone before, you may want to offer credit terms to encourage retailers to buy from you. Many woodworkers will insist on cash while they are starting their business, then add credit terms when they are ready to expand. Figure 5-4 is a typical credit application.

Woodworker Rick Rochon of Olor Enterprises offers three credit terms: cash with order, collect on delivery (COD) or on account. His shipper will collect on delivery for a small fee, which Rick tacks on to the price of the order. In establishing an account, Rick requires three credit references. He may or may not verify the references, depending on the size of the first order. His theory is, "Who would give me a bad credit reference?"

Other Sales Opportunities

You can apply your creativity to where and how you sell your woodworking. Though most arts and crafts are sold through retail outlets, galleries and craft shows, many other opportunities exist for selling your woodworking.

Depending on the type of woodworking product you produce, you can display samples at non-traditional retail and service businesses. For example, you can ask your banker to allow you to display your woodworking in their window or on a counter. Or you can suggest that they promote the local arts and purchase some of your woodworking products for their lobby or even as gifts to their best customers. Another excellent location to display or sell your works is at area restaurants. Family restaurants may appreciate having old-fashioned decorations or even antique reproductions in their waiting area.

As you contact these businesses, ask for the owner or manager, explain that you are a local woodworker and suggest specific products that would look good in their business. Ask them if the business would buy some of your products; if not, can you display them at the business?

Other locations where you may be able to sell or display your woodworking products include attorney, accountant, doctor and other professional offices; libraries; corporate offices; and municipal buildings.

How much should you pay a salesperson for selling your woodworking products? The standard commission for craft sales is 15 percent of retail or wholesale price, depending on to whom they sell. A distributor takes on some marketing responsibilities and sometimes warehouses a product it sells. For this, the typical distributor gets a 35 percent commission.

Consignment Selling

Selling wholesale to retail stores is a popular alternative to sitting at a craft show all weekend. Finding retail outlets for your woodworking products can make life much easier. However, while some retailers will pay in advance or within 30 days of delivery, others will want your products on consignment. Should you consign your products? That depends.

Woodshop News reported that 27 percent of all

craft shops surveyed report that they carry most of their work on consignment. Another 19 percent take some wood crafts on consignment — mostly larger pieces — and purchase the rest.

How Consignment Works

Under a typical consignment deal, you let the retailer display your product without buying it. They pay you only when they sell the product. Consignment shops typically pay from 50 to 70 percent of retail. That is, if they sell your $100 woodworking product, they will pay you between $50 and $70. As an average, they will pay you about two-thirds of the retail price and keep one-third for their efforts. You earn an extra 17 percent of the retail price (34 percent of the wholesale price). You also take the risk that the product won't sell or that, if sold, the retailer won't pay you as promised. Some woodworkers simply increase their wholesale prices to compensate for the risk. Others limit their consignments to a percentage of all sales. Some will offer products on consignment only to outlets that they want to develop as primary customers. Still other woodworkers refuse to sell any products on consignment. Experience will teach you what works.

Record Keeping Is Important

Consignment selling is more common with artistic wood products sold through art dealers, but can be used to sell any type of woodworking product. It requires that you keep accurate and complete records on every piece you consign, that you require a signature on delivery and that you set a time limit on the consignment. Some merchants will move consignment pieces to the back room if they don't sell quickly. They want to first sell the products that they have purchased. A typical consignment period is 90 to 180 days.

Alternatives

But what if you don't want to sell on consignment and the store doesn't want to buy it for cash? You have some alternatives. You can require cash on delivery but offer a return policy if it hasn't sold within 90 to 180 days. Of course, you will have to carefully watch your checkbook as the return of a large shipment can take the balance down fast. Or you can offer your first sale to a new customer on consignment, but require that reorders be on cash or 30-day terms.

Setting Up a Showroom

You may decide that, because of the size of your woodworking products and the proximity of most of your customers, you can sell from a showroom. Large furniture or cabinetry is an example. The showroom may be a room of your home, an addition to your shop, outdoors or even a retail location where you can display your works. Such a showroom gives you greater control over how your woodworking products are shown and how the customer is sold. This may seem like an ideal situation for a woodworker. However, in most cases, a showroom becomes an expensive sales tool that can take many hours away from your first love: woodworking. Here are some proven alternatives.

If your products show best in a showroom, search for another woodworker who has or needs a showroom and split the costs and work. You can also gather numerous woodworking or crafts products from other artisans and offer to display their works to help cover your costs.

Another option is to set aside a small room in your home for showing but open it only during specified hours, such as weekends or certain evenings. Or ask a family member to maintain the showroom for you.

A word of warning: Do not undersell your retail clients. If you make wooden boxes that retail for $100 and you wholesale them for $50 to gift shops in your area, don't sell them directly to the public for $70. If you must sell locally, sell for the same price that your retail clients get. A single under-priced sale can cost you a valuable wholesale client.

Finding a Sales Representative

The job of a sales representative is to trade some of your headaches for some of your money. He or she can take over the task of selling what you make and give you time to make more. It can be a good investment or an even bigger headache.

A sales representative can be your exclusive sales agent, or sell only in a region of the country, or sell only a few of your products. It's up to you. Some woodworkers find sales reps for regions of the country that they can't cover. Then, as the business grows, they offer their local region as a sales territory to the same or another sales rep.

Paying the Sales Rep

How much does a sales rep get paid? That depends on what the rep does for you. Some will spend much time representing you at wholesale shows, taking your products into retail stores, sending out brochures and price sheets, and making sure that your products are being displayed well. Others will throw a couple of your samples in their bag as they travel from store to store. Most reps are paid by commission, a percentage of what they sell. The exact percentage depends on what they do to earn the fee and at what price they sell the product. It may also depend on how much they sell during a given period. Commissions may change as sales volume changes. One sales rep may receive only a 5 percent commission of retail price. Another may earn as much as 30 percent of retail for his or her efforts. Typical sales commissions are in the mid-dle: 10 to 20 percent of retail. However, the rep may cost you little or nothing by getting a higher wholesale price for your woodworking products.

Selling by Mail

Many woodworkers have successfully sold their products by mail. Shipping costs can limit the size of woodworking products sold by mail, but the primary limiting factor is often price. The shipping cost per sale can be $5 to $50 depending on the item, so the product is usually not an $8 item. If it is, it's one that will encourage customers to buy more from the seller. On the other end, it is difficult to sell products for over about $100 by mail unless the firm's reputation has been built to the level of an L.L. Bean or a Neiman Marcus.

One successful woodworker lives on the Oregon coast, yet sells his products across the nation. He depends extensively on shipping services to allow him to deliver his products anywhere within just a few days of an order. "I sell very few of my products locally. If it weren't for UPS I'd be out of business." He established accounts with major shipping services and set up a "shipping table" in his shop. Each day the drivers stop by to pick up any outgoing packages.

Marketing by Mail

Woodworkers who sell by mail will use printed postcards, brochures or mini catalogs to send information on their products to prospective customers. A woodworker making wooden toys can produce a four-color catalog sheet for about $500 and mail it to craft stores, gift shops, children's shops or families with younger children. Depending on the quality of the list, about 2 percent of the recipients will order.

Mail-order sales campaigns can get quite expensive. If you plan to use this method of selling your

Creative Woodcraft Inc.

Shipping

123 Main Street, Yourtown USA 12345

Trailer/ Car Number	Bill Date
45678	March 1, 2005

TO

CONSIGNEE
Harrison Gallery

STREET
876 Main St.

DESTINATION
Receiving Dept.

CITY	STATE	ZIP
Anothertown	AN	16543

Route:

FROM

SHIPPER
Creative Woodcraft, Inc

STREET
123 Main St.

ORIGIN

CITY	STATE	ZIP
Yourtown	AN	12345

Special Instructions:

FOR PAYMENT, SEND BILL TO

NAME
same as above

COMPANY

STREET

CITY   STATE   ZIP

Shipper's Internal Data

No. Shipping Units	Time	Description of Articles, Special Marks and Exceptions	Weight	Rate	Charges
1		36" x 48" custom frame of oak and rosewood	17 lb.	3.10	52.70

REMIT C.O.D.
TO:
ADDRESS:
NOTE: Where the rate is dependent on value, shippers are required to state specifically in writing the agreed or declared value of the property. The agreed or declared value of the property is hereby specifically stated by the shipper to be not exceeding
$ per

COD AMOUNT: $
If this shipment is to be delivered to the consignee without recourse on the consignor, the consignor shall sign the following statement:
The carrier shall not make delivery of this shipment without payment of freight and all other lawful charges.

(Signature of Consignor)

C.O.D FEE
PREPAID ☐
COLLECT ☐

TOTAL CHARGES $ 52.70

Freight Charges are collect unless marked prepaid
CHECK BOX IF PREPAID ☒

RECEIVED subject to the classifications and tariffs in effect on the date of the issue of this Bill of Lading, the property described above in apparent good order, except as noted (contents and condition of contents of packages unknown), marked consigned and destined as indicated above which said carrier (the word carrier being understood through this contract as meaning any person or corporation in possession of the property under the contract) agrees to carry to its usual place of delivery as said destination. If on its route, otherwise to deliver to another carrier on the route to said destination. It is mutually agreed as to each carrier of all or any of said property,over all or any portion of said route to destination and as to each party at any time interested in all or any said property, that every service to be performed hereunder shall be subject to all the Bill of Lading terms and conditions in the governing classification on the date of shipment. Shipper hereby certifies that he is familiar with all the Bill of Lading terms and conditions in the governing classification and the said terms and conditions are hereby agreed to by the shipper and accepted for himself and his assigns.

Shipper   Carrier
Per   Per   Date:

Figure 5-5. Here is a typical Shipping document. A blank form that you can reproduce and use is included in the appendix.

woodworking, look for a direct-mail consultant who will help you develop a profitable campaign. A consultant will charge a fee, but will typically save you money or earn you sufficient sales to cover their costs. However, most direct-mail consultants won't work on campaigns smaller than a few thousand dollars in total costs. The alternative is to learn as much as you can about direct mail and copywriting, then design your own mail-order system for selling your woodworking products.

Another alternative is to cooperate with non-competing woodworkers in a direct-mail campaign and split the costs. You may even find woodworkers in your group who have direct-mail or mail-order experience.

Product Dealers

Woodworkers can sell their products by mail through mail-order product dealers. The dealer may specialize in gift items or personalized items. Approach them as you would a retail outlet, with samples and ideas. Some mail-order outlets will require that you be able to produce a specific number of units within a short time, so be ready to do so if you want their order. They don't want to sell 4,000 of your turned candleholders if you can produce only four a day.

If you decide to develop a mail-order business, do some research to find the best way of shipping your products to customers. Depending on what you sell, to whom and where they are located, you may select the postal service, a package delivery service, an overnight service or even a freight service. Check your area phone books under "Delivery Service," "Shipping" or "Mailing Services." If you live in a rural area or most of your customers do, you may be limited in the delivery services offered. Even so, any service you select will help you determine how best to package and ship your products for safe arrival in a timely manner. Figure 5-5 illustrates a typical shipping form.

Selling Commissioned Art

Some woodworkers find their niche at the high end. They sell their woodworking products to those who will pay for unique artistry purchased directly from the artist. Their clients are large corporations, corporate executives, foundations, art connoisseurs, art patrons, museums and public art galleries. Each piece is designed for and commissioned by the particular client.

Shop Rate

The shop rate for commissioned art is higher than for other woodworking crafts — often between $60 and $100 an hour — but so is the risk. Artisans who sell commissioned work typically have a tested system for establishing and collecting fees. They have developed business experience, have sold woodworking crafts, have earned name recognition through awards and have a lawyer-written contract requiring deposits and payments. Few woodworkers start at this level, but most aspire to it.

Commissioned woodworking projects are typically paid for in two or three installments. The first installment should be made when the commission is accepted and the project is outlined. A letter from you to the purchaser describing the project and the payment terms can serve as a basic contract. Depending on the size of the project, the length of time required and your negotiating skills, you may receive the second installment at a specific point in the project or at the end when it is delivered. Some woodworkers establish a three-payment plan to help with their own cash flow.

Knowing Your Customers

Who buys your woodworking products? Why? What do you know about them? How do they use your products? How often do they need to replace your product? How will they select a replacement? Where do they buy your product? Will these customers look somewhere else for your type of product? What do they expect to pay for similar products?

Lots of questions. But only by asking these types of questions will you learn more about your customers and what they want. How can you learn the answers to these and related questions about your customers? By asking. When? Anytime you can.

For example, one successful wooden-clock maker sells most of her products at large open-air flea markets in a metropolitan area. Sometimes her booth is quite busy with sales and other times it isn't. She uses the slower times to ask questions of people who stop at the booth: Have you ever purchased one of my clocks? Do you have any wooden clocks at home? What design do you prefer? What do you like about wooden clocks? Do you prefer one wood species over another? She asks each of the people who buy a clock from her the same question: What attracted you to that particular wooden clock? From her conversations with customers, she has modified her design twice and added a line of smaller and less-expensive clocks. She took the time to learn about her customers and what they want. She now works full-time at making and selling her wooden clocks.

Tailoring Your Product to Demand

Once you know who your typical customer is — what he buys, how and where he buys, how much he expects to pay, on what terms, and what related woodworking products he might buy — you can clone your customer. You can search for similar people and help them understand the features and benefits of your woodworking products.

A successful custom-cabinet maker asked enough questions of his customers to learn that many were executives transferring in from other locations and upgrading homes they found in the rustic community. So he talked with local reloca-

tion services, moving companies, real estate agents and major employers about his services. He supplied them with business cards, brochures and letters of reference. He checked back monthly with his better contacts to determine if any transfers were expected. As appropriate, he would then send a brochure and letter to the person being transferred. His brochure included references from past customers the transferee may know at the same firm. By learning about his customers he was able to find new ones.

Building Repeat and Referral Business

Customers are hard to find and harder to keep. The price of finding new customers can be a burden on a small business. Advertising for new business can eat up 10 to 25 percent of your sales dollars. Finding and exhibiting at new craft shows can be expensive, as well. What do other successful woodworkers do about this problem? They build repeat and referral business.

Repeat Business

Repeat business is simply sales to your current customers. You can sell them more of the same products, related products or even new products. Or you can sell them all the above.

For example, rather than spend excessive time developing new customers, one successful wooden-toy maker kept contacting existing customers with new toy designs. He photographed his new creations, pasted the photos on a sheet of paper, hand-lettered information and pricing about the new product, had color copies made at a neighborhood copy shop, and mailed them to his current customers. Depending on the design and product, he sold these toys to as many as 40 percent of his existing customers. His sales costs were less than a dollar per unit. He is now developing a marketing idea to offer a toy-of-the-month club with 12 different toys throughout the year. He's hoping that grandparents will subscribe for their grandchildren. His sales costs will be low and he will be able to smooth out his business's cash flow because he is developing repeat business.

Referral Business

You can also reduce sales costs and increase profits by developing referral business. That is, you ask your customers to bring you new customers. The cost is minimal and the opportunities are great. As current customers praise your work, you ask if they know of anyone who might also enjoy your products. Make it a habit to ask. Then, as you contact these referrals, be sure to mention that the customer referred you. Of course, make sure you first have permission from the current customer to do so. Depending on the product you sell, you can offer a reward to your current customer for any new customers they bring you. If you sell kitchen cabinets, you can give customers a kitchen tool or related item for referring you to others. Or you can offer a small discount on the next project you do for them. Do whatever it takes to appropriately thank your customers for the referral and to encourage them to refer others to you.

Remember to scatter your business cards and brochures widely. They cannot help you build repeat and referral business if they live in your desk. Make sure that you have them in your presentation binder, your toolbox, your vehicle's glove compartment and even your jacket pocket. You never know when or where you'll get a chance to develop repeat and referral business.

When to Increase Prices

As your woodworking venture grows, you have two options:

1. Make more product, or
2. Make more money.

For many part-time woodworking ventures, the first action is to make more product. That is, the part-time woodturning venture becomes a full-time business. This may be exactly what you want to do — or it may not. You may prefer to do your woodworking on a part-time basis, making a profit on it but not giving up what you do the rest of the time, whether it's work a full-time job or golfing and fishing.

So you take the second option: Make more money by increasing your shop or hourly rate. You might decide to go from $35 an hour to $40 an hour for all products you make after a specific date, say July 1. Or you can increase your profit margin. Or you can maintain your shop rate but try for a higher wholesale or retail price.

Don't Sell Yourself Short

Remember, too many woodworker hobbyists sell their talents short. That is, they underprice their work and undervalue their skills. Learn to realistically price your woodworking projects and you will ensure that you get to do what you love.

To increase your prices, decide what your new pricing should be, calculate how it will impact your unit prices, set a date for the increase and then be flexible.

Don Meisner built outdoor furniture from pressure-treated woods. He built most of his units on the weekends, primarily on Saturday to allow most of Sunday for family. About a year after he began, Don was working at least 10 hours on Saturday and 4 on Sunday — and still getting behind on orders. He had a potential contract with a regional hardware-store chain that, combined with his other business, could give him a total of 25 hours of work a week. He could almost take his woodworking venture into a full-time business.

Instead, Don decided to not bid on the hardware chain contract until he had more business experience. Rather, he decided to increase his shop rate by 25 percent — from $40 to $50 an hour. Because most of his sales were directly to the customers and labor was one-half of his price, this meant a 12.5 percent increase in his retail prices. An $120 settee now became $135. This change didn't reduce his sales, but it gave him the funds to employ his teenage daughter on Saturdays as a shop assistant. Don was back to one weekend workday per week and had the chance to spend it with a member of his family. After his daughter's graduation — if she still enjoys woodworking — Don plans to bid on wholesale jobs to give his family extra income and a chance to work at home.

Outsourcing Specialized Work

Taking on a woodworking project may require that you use a specialized tool or process, such as needing turned spindles for dinette chairs you're making. Rather than purchasing the necessary lathe, gouges and related turning tools, you can "outsource" this work. That is, you can find another woodworker who has these tools and will produce the needed components to your specifications and standards. You will save money, as well as help another woodworker make money at his or her craft.

If you prefer to do the work yourself, you may find a woodworking shop that will let you rent their equipment to produce the needed parts. This

has a liability issue: Whose insurance covers you if you are injured using their equipment? Discuss this possibility with your insurance agent and make sure everyone understands what you're paying for.

Outsourcing specialized work is an especially profitable solution if you find yourself with a woodworking contract that you just can't complete on deadline. You may have the right equipment, but not enough hours in the day. You can then select a component of your work, such as preparing blanks for turning or building cabinet shelves, that you subcontract to another woodworker. Of course, the time to select a subcontractor is before you need them. Know who else works with wood in your area, what they do, their skill level and their attitude toward quality. Inspect some of their work. Then, when the big job comes in, you're ready to bid and fulfill it because you have resources.

Start a Cooperative

The idea of outsourcing specialized work leads to another opportunity you should consider: a woodworker's cooperative. Woodworkers who don't compete with each other can reduce costs and potentially increase income by renting a large shop together and sharing some equipment and jobs. For example, a woodturner and a woodcarver could establish a cooperative shop that they share. It would include a single radial-arm saw rather than two, because they don't use it as often. The shop may instead have both a band saw and a jigsaw for cutting blocks and patterns. The co-op shop can go together to hire a part-time bookkeeper and even a salesperson to jointly sell their woodworking products.

The advantages to a woodworker's cooperative are clear. The downside is that maintaining a balanced partnership is often difficult. What if the cooperating woodworker gets busy and can't help you with your projects? What if you can afford to replace an important power tool but the cooperating woodworker cannot? Woodworker's co-ops work; but they also require work.

Bidding a Job

Depending on what type of woodworking you do, you may be asked to produce a large quantity of a single component for another woodworker, sell your product exclusively to a single source or develop a bid. A bid is simply a written offer to perform a job at a specified price. A bid may also be called a quote, a price quotation or a proposal. A change is made with a change order. In each case, once it is accepted and signed, it is a legally binding document.

Get Bid Instructions

If you learn of an invitation to bid, contact the firm or representative letting the bid and ask for bid instructions. These are rules under which your bid must be submitted. Ask when the bids will be opened and the job let. It will also be helpful if you can find a sample form on which to submit your bid. The more you know before you calculate and write your bid, the better chance you have of being a successful bidder. Figure 5-6 illustrates a bid quotation.

A bid record is simply a written record of bids prepared and submitted. It gives you the opportunity to track your success as a bidder and to determine whether specific competitors are taking too much business from you.

Depending on the size of the bid, you may be required to post a bid security, typically a certified check or performance bond, to ensure that if you are the successful bidder, you will perform the service as contracted. If you're not a successful bidder, your security will be returned to you. If the firm you're bidding to requires a performance bond, discuss it with your insurance agent.

Types of Bids

Bids can take many forms, including labor only, time and materials, fixed price, unit price, cost plus and guaranteed minimum. Let's define each one briefly.

LABOR ONLY

The woodworker furnishes labor, tools and equipment, and the customer furnishes materials. The labor charge includes the cost of labor, taxes/benefits, overhead and a profit.

TIME AND MATERIALS

Labor is billed at hourly service rates established for each worker, and material is billed at retail price (sometimes less a discount). Overhead costs are built into the labor rates. Profit comes from the hourly service rates, as well as from the sale of materials.

FIXED PRICE

The total price includes the cost of materials, labor, direct job expenses, prorated overhead costs, and profit.

UNIT PRICE

Total price is broken down into components: labor, job expenses, overhead, and profit on units of material.

COST PLUS FEE

The costs of materials, labor and job expenses are reimbursed at actual cost, plus a fee to cover overhead and profit.

COST PLUS PERCENTAGE

The costs of materials, labor and job expenses are reimbursed at actual cost, plus a percentage to cover overhead and profit.

GUARANTEED MINIMUM

The total lump-sum price is guaranteed with the

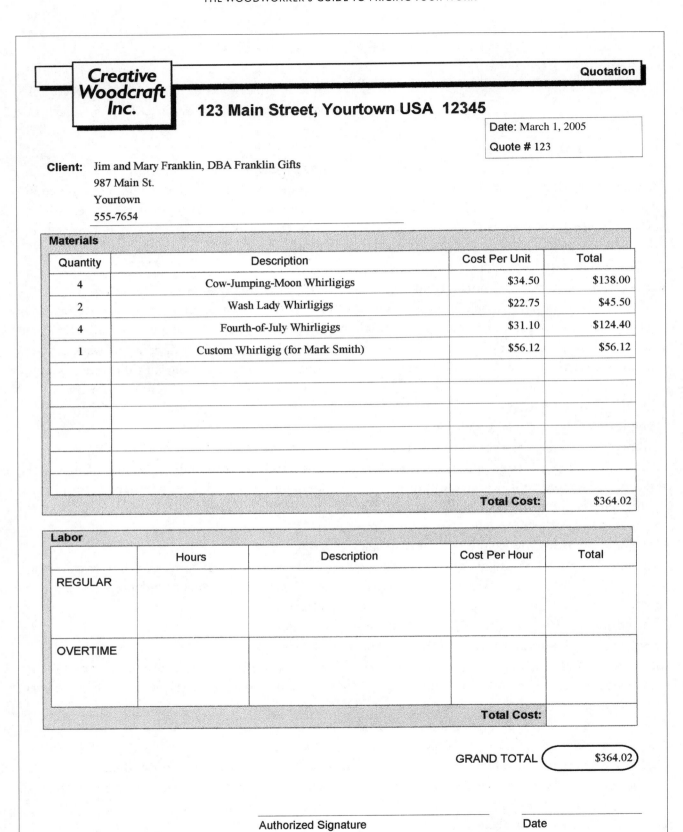

Figure 5-6. Use this Quotation form to bid on a woodworking project's materials and labor. A blank form that you can reproduce and use is included in the appendix.

assurance that, if final costs are under the limit, the savings will be split.

Payment Terms

What payment terms should you include in your bid? Here are some common payment schedules:

- 100 percent due on completion of the work
- 50 percent at midpoint in the job and 50 percent on completion
- 20 percent down, with scheduled progress payment throughout the job (20 percent when one-fourth, one-half, three-fourths and fully done)
- Bill the first of every month for work completed during the previous month

Subcontracting to another woodworker or selling exclusively to a single buyer can reduce both your risks and your profit. Make sure you can pay expenses and still make a profit with your bid.

Reducing Material Costs

Materials used in woodworking are a major component of your costs. Your woodworking enterprise can increase profits if you can find a way of reducing material costs. Here are some proven ideas you can use to cut the cost of materials.

Andy Peterson builds small birdhouses from pine he buys through a local lumber retailer. After a year of building birdhouses and selling them at weekend craft fairs in his region, Andy determined which models sold best and projected how many he could expect to sell in the coming year. He then set up an account with a wholesaler and purchased his materials in quantity twice a year. The wholesaler allowed Andy to pay for the materials over a 90-day period. By managing his cash flow (covered earlier in this chapter), Andy reduced his materials costs by over 20 percent and made his woodworking business more profitable.

What if Andy didn't have any idea how much material he would use in the coming year? Or what if Andy didn't have the cash to buy six months' worth of materials at a time? He has other options — and so do you.

Buying in Quantity

Woodworkers can reduce material costs by cooperating with other woodworkers to buy in quantity. This is an especially effective technique for woodworkers who need exotic woods and better-grade hardwoods such as oak. Quantity purchase of these woods can reduce their cost by as much as 50 percent without reducing quality. By learning as much as you can about other woodworkers in your area, their products and their material needs, you can often find someone who orders your types of materials in larger quantities and who will tack your order onto theirs. It may help them get a better price, as well. Expect to pay a small fee for this service. Or if the materials must be picked up, you can offer to pick up and deliver them in exchange for the benefits of including your needs on the order.

Networking with Other Woodworkers

You should know as much as you can about other woodworkers in your area and even your region of the country. By doing so, you may find additional opportunities for reducing material costs. In our example, Andy could also reduce costs by finding a woodworker who has scrap materials Andy can use. He found an excellent price break on pine, but couldn't earn a discount on redwood he wanted for the roofs of his birdhouses. But he found something better — a cedar shake mill in his state that sold him smaller pieces he needed for scrap prices. Every few months, Andy drove to the factory for a pickup load. By reducing overall material costs by approximately 35 percent, Andy has been able to maintain workmanship while reducing his prices to meet new competition.

You can't produce high-quality woodworking

products without using quality supplies and materials. It's also hard to meet deadlines if materials aren't delivered when promised and in the quantity and quality promised.

Finding Suppliers

Where can you find the right supplier? One way is by recommendations from other woodworkers. Another is through advertisements in magazines like *American Woodworker*, *Fine Woodworking*, *Popular Woodworking*, *Woodworker's Journal*, *Weekend Woodcrafts*, *Wood*, *Woodshop News*, *Woodwork*, *Woodworker*, *Workbench* and others. For each potential supplier you want to know what supplies and materials they have available, their pricing and discounts, delivery costs and terms, return policy and minimum order requirements. You will also want to learn how knowledgeable and helpful they are. Do they understand woodworking, or are they just a store?

If you find two suppliers that are approximately equal sources, use them both. Then you have an alternative source if prices go up. Or you may decide to give all your business to the better supplier in exchange for an additional discount. In any case, always have an alternate supplier that you can use if your primary supplier doesn't serve you well.

Upgrading Tools and Equipment

When should you upgrade your equipment? Whenever you can make more money by doing so. Rick Rochon of Olor Enterprises (www.olor.net) makes photo albums, selling them wholesale to gift shops across the nation. Rick says the best advice given to him is: Invest in quality primary equipment. To invest in equipment means that it must make you more money than it costs. If a new

$2,000 lathe will pay for itself in a year in labor or expenses saved, buy it now. Don't wait. However, if it will be used only an hour or two a week, hold off and invest in equipment that will save or make more money.

Rick also recommends that woodworkers invest in the best equipment they can afford. If a good sander will pay for itself in six months and a high-quality sander will take eight months, buy quality. Once it's paid off, it will make you as much money, but it will do so longer.

Tax Deductions

Current tax laws allow businesses to expense up to $100,000 in equipment each year. That is, rather than depreciate or spread the cost of a new saw over three years, you can deduct it as a legitimate expense for the year it is purchased. That's money you won't have to pay taxes on. For example, if you purchase a $3,000 saw and write it off as an expense, and you are now paying 35 percent of your profit for taxes, the saw cost you just $1,950; Uncle Sam indirectly paid the rest. Of course, you must make sure you will show a profit before you spend it. And you must make sure that the equipment will more than pay for itself. Consult with a tax professional before buying major equipment to make sure you get the greatest tax benefit.

Making Your Shop More Efficient

The key to a higher shop rate is higher efficiency. That is, as you learn how to do more in less time you will earn more.

Convenience and Space Needs

You can make your shop more efficient in many ways. First, make sure your shop is convenient.

That is, if you do woodworking only two or three hours in the evening, don't locate your shop across town. Instead, keep it at your home as long as you can. If you need more space, consider expanding your shop or even building a separate materials-storage area to give you more work space.

How much space you need depends on what you make. A cabinetmaker typically requires at least 400 square feet (20' × 20') of shop space. A woodworker making children's toys may need only 240 square feet (12' × 20') of shop space for tools, materials and inventory. A whittler may use as little as 25 square feet (5' × 5') for tools and materials. Of course, allow additional space for tools that you own but don't frequently use in making your primary wood craft product.

Another factor in estimating needed shop space is determining how many people will work in the shop at a time. For most woodworkers, the answer is easy: one. But if you're building your part-time venture with the help of a friend or relative, you may need more space.

To ensure that your shop will be efficient, make sure you have adequate electrical, lighting, heating and other services. Depending on your power tool requirements, you may need 220V service, as well as 110V. Plan for the future.

Design Work Areas for Efficiency

You can make your shop more efficient by grouping tools and work areas by function. That is, if you cut and rout panels into doors, locate your radial-arm saw and your router near each other with sufficient room for storing materials between procedures. Jim Tolpin's *Measure Twice, Cut Once* (Popular Woodworking Books, 1993, 1996) outlines numerous simple yet effective ways of reducing waste.

Efficient shop production means making the fewest inefficient moves. It means planning your work so that material from a completed process is placed where it is easily available for the next process. That is, a door panel that is cut to size is then placed in a stack that can be reached from the router station. That makes sense, but many woodworkers who have not done much production work will stack, then restack, components.

To make sure that your woodworking process is efficient, list the steps required for producing your product, then review it for efficiency of movement. For example, your process may require a written work order with specific measurements of the finished product. If so, include a space for listing the dimensions of each component. If possible, list them in the order of production, such as cabinet frames, doors, hardware, then tops. By doing so, you'll make sure that you work efficiently as well as minimize waste.

An excellent resource for learning from other woodworking shops is the *Woodshop News* (10 Bokum Road, Essex, CT 06426; 860-767-8227; www.woodshopnews.com). It includes designs of jigs and fixtures, woodworking industry news and new products, and articles on the business side of woodworking.

Shop Safety

In order to become a successful woodworker you must not be folded, spindled or mutilated by your tools. Make sure you wear protective goggles or safety glasses, and have a sealed first-aid kit and a few ABC fire extinguishers handy.

If you hire employees, remember that they must be covered by workers' compensation insurance and that your shop must meet OSHA (Occupational Safety and Health Administration) safety requirements. Also, employees or not, make sure you have adequate insurance to cover accidents.

SIX

Profitably Using Technology

Technology is considered by some woodworkers to be a curse word. After all, isn't woodworking about using your hands and simple tools to carefully craft works of art? How does technology play a part in the woodworker's skills and shop?

By definition, woodworking is technology. Techno is derived from a Greek word meaning "art" or "skill"; consider the related word *technique*. The *ology* part of the word is from the Greek for "knowledge." So knowledge about an art or skill, such as woodworking, is technology.

What's typically meant today by the word *technology* is electronic or computer technology. The perception is that using computer technology in woodworking homogenizes the artistic elements. It can make woodworking uniform and without character. Mass production is simply technology over-applied to art. Every piece of furniture, every turned bowl looks the same as the last and next. Designs are simplified to meet the requirements of computerized production.

Is there a balance? Can the craftsperson use technology to actually enhance artistic value, as well as increase profitability?

Yes!

That's what this chapter is about: profitably using technology to share your artistic gifts and skills with others. In fact, you can use computer technology in many ways to increase profitability outside of your creative process. You can use computers to help price and sell your woodworking.

This chapter shows you how to select computer hardware and software that will increase woodworking profits. It will describe the opportunities available to you on the Internet for researching, buying and selling your craft. It will even show you how to set up and run your own profitable Web site and introduce you to those who have. Then this chapter will describe how you can select and use computerized tools to take over the mundane tasks and allow you to give more artistic time to your products. Finally, you'll see how other technologies can increase your woodworking profits.

Sound exciting?

A note: Maybe you've already dabbled into computers, the Internet and computerized woodworking tools. Even so, within this chapter you will find tips and techniques for applying new ideas.

Let's get started.

About Computers and Hardware

Personal computers, or PCs, haven't been around very long compared to most woodworking tools. Though universities and big businesses have been using computers for about five decades, the personal or desktop computer is now more than 25 years old, and the Internet is just over 10 years old — and growing fast .

So what is a computer? It is a machine. This machine is made to follow instructions given to it. The instructions tell it what to do with provided information. The machine is the hardware. The instructions are the software. The information is the data. That's a computer in a nutshell.

For example, a PC has software installed that will format or process words. The software is called a word processor. The data is the words that you type on your computer's keyboard. The software can select the size of the letters, width of the lines and spacing between lines; count the words; change the font or look of the letters; and even check spelling against a dictionary (also software). It even can help you edit for proper grammar. Actually, all it's doing is following instructions previously written by a programmer.

The PC may take up a couple of cubic feet on your desk, but the brain of the computer is a small chip inside (smaller than a cracker) called a central processing unit, or CPU. Everything else inside your computer helps the CPU get the job done. The keyboard and mouse are input tools. So is the CD-ROM. The monitor that displays text is an output. So is the printer. The modem hardware that gets you on to the Internet is an input/output, or I/O, tool. The hard drive is a storage tool because it stores both the software and your data. The random-access memory, or RAM, is a temporary "workbench" where the software works on the data.

One more critical piece to the computer puzzle is the operating system, or OS. You've probably heard of Windows, Macintosh, Linux and maybe a few other OSs. The OS is software that translates between application software (word processors, for example) and the computer's hardware. The critical thing to remember is that application software (apps) written for Microsoft Windows OS won't work on other OS machines, such as Linux. So you must buy apps designed for the OS. But note that Microsoft offers versions of their software for the Macintosh and that many Mac programs have Windows versions.

See, you're already getting into computer lingo!

Want some more? Let's look at an ad for a PC and figure out what it's saying:

Operating System: Microsoft Windows XP (operating system that translates apps to the hardware)

CPU: Intel Pentium 4 3.2 GHz (brand, model, and speed of CPU; GHz is gigahertz or one billion cycles per second)

Memory or RAM: 512 MB 400 MHz (the amount of random-access memory included and the storage speed at which it reads and writes data; MB is a million data pieces, and MHz is a million cycles per second)

Hard Drive: 80 GB (size of storage area: 6 billion pieces of data)

Diskette: 3.5" 1.44 MB (portable storage disk for installing software and saving data)

CD: 48X (maximum reading speed; a CD holds about 680 MB of data)

DVD: 16X (maximum reading speed; a DVD holds about 4.4 GB of data)

Modem: V90 56K (56K, or 56,000 bytes per second, is the fastest speed)

Sound: Sound Blaster (a sound card translates data files into sounds)

Expansion Slots: 3 PCI available (three slots available for adding other hardware)

Ports: 2 USB, 1 serial, 1 parallel, 2 RJ-11, mouse and keyboard, monitor (ports are used to connect to other hardware such as printer, scanner and mouse)

Mouse: USB (universal serial bus connection, 12 to 80 MB/second)

Keyboard: USB or wireless (wireless uses radio waves to transmit data)

It's probably starting to get confusing. I think it's intended to be so. Consider this: A computer and related software are simply tools, just as are saws, sanders and squares. You learn about them as you use them. And you don't buy them until you know how you will use them. So, as you learn more about computer technology and its tools, think about how you can apply these tools. As a rule of thumb, you will select computer technology tools by first selecting the software that fits the solution, then choosing the OS and hardware required by the software.

One other question you might ask: Are computers expensive? That depends on what you think "expensive" is. The computer described above, produced by a major manufacturer, is plenty fast for most small businesses. The cost is less than $1,000. If you're willing to take last year's technology, you can cut the price in half.

Useful Software

Now that you understand the basics of computers, you can better see how computer programs or software work for you. And even though computer hardware is discussed first, you will probably select the software tools before you choose the computer and OS to run it on.

Useful software includes drawing, writing, accounting and database programs. Following is a quick overview of each. Visit a local computer store for more information.

CAD

Many useful computer-aided drafting, or CAD, software programs are available today. They are quite useful for drawing plans for woodworking projects. All require either a mouse or a drawing pad for input. The drawing tool is used to draw lines and shapes, move objects, identify components and even add colors to the drawing.

Popular entry-level CAD programs include various versions of Autodesk (www.autodesk.com) and Microsoft Visio (www.microsoft.com/office/visio), a drawing and diagramming program.

Word Processor

If you write a business plan, send a letter to prospects or customers, write an advertisement or write to suppliers, you may want a word processor software program. Word processors simply process words. That is, they let you type words into the computer, move them around, insert words, take some out and make any changes before you print them on paper. I've use word processors for more than 20 years and would never go back to typewriters. Word processors let you change your mind.

Common word processing programs include Microsoft Word (www.microsoft.com/office/word) and Corel WordPerfect (www.wordperfect.com). At one time there were many more, but the acceptance of MS Word by business has made it a standard.

Accounting

To track your business's expenses, use one of the popular accounting programs such as Microsoft Money (www.microsoft.com/money), Intuit Quicken (www.quicken.com) and its big brother QuickBooks (www.quickbooks.com), and Peachtree Complete Accounting (www.peachtree.com). These and other programs replace your check register. In fact, they also can be used to print your checks. When entering a check you also enter the income or expense category. It's a little more work than simply writing in a paper checkbook, but it pays off. Reconciling a bank statement — typically a frustrating and time-consuming job when done manually — takes just a few minutes each month. And income taxes are simpler to calculate from easy-to-run reports. In fact, income tax software can import data from these checking programs, saving you even more time. You also can pay your bills electronically using these programs – no checks to print!

The key to using computer accounting programs is similar to the woodworking adage, "Plan twice, enter once." Carefully setting up your income and expense categories and entering each transaction will give you accurate reports and easier taxes. It also can give you a better understanding of where your profits (or losses) are coming from.

In addition to checking software, spreadsheet software can be useful to your woodworking business. A spreadsheet arranges numbers into useable form. It's named after the wide multicolumnar sheets that accountants use to make journal entries. You can use spreadsheet programs in many ways.

As an example, a basic spreadsheet program (available for less than $100) lets you enter horizontal rows of job expense categories and vertical columns of numbers in cells. Most important, you can then instruct the program to make calculations on any or all the cells and it will do so in less than a second. And if you update a number, the program automatically recalculates the totals for you. Many spreadsheet programs can follow instructions you write, called macros, to do special calculations automatically. For example, a macro can select all of the invoices over 60 days due and total them up, or give you the percentage of their total versus all invoices. Better spreadsheets will also produce fancy graphs and pie charts that make reports easier to understand. They impress lenders and other financial types, too.

The most popular spreadsheet program is Microsoft Excel (www.microsoft.com/excel/). Lotus 1-2-3 is available as a component of Lotus SmartSuite (www.lotus.com).

Database

Why would a woodworker ever need database software? A database is much like an index card file box. You can store thousands of pieces of information. But a database program is even better than a file box because it finds information in the files in a fraction of a second.

The most common application of a database program for a woodworking business is inventory. You can use a database to keep track of stock as you buy it, what you paid for it, and how it was used. You can link the database to a spreadsheet to determine if the stock was profitable. In addition, a database is useful for keeping track of customers, suppliers and other resources.

The most popular database programs include Microsoft Access (www.microsoft.com/access), Lotus Approach (www.lotus.com) and FileMaker (www.filemaker.com).

Integrated Programs

Fortunately, you can also find integrated software programs that combine the primary programs: word processor, spreadsheet and database. Some packages include other related programs such as

Internet browsers. One advantage of integrated software is that they operate similarly, so once you learn one you're halfway to learning the others. As important, integrated packages are less expensive than individual programs.

For example, Microsoft Office (www.office.microsoft.com) includes integrated word processor, spreadsheet, database and other tools, depending on which edition you get. Corel WordPerfect Office includes a similar package.

Other Programs

Computer software tools have been written to solve many small business problems. For example, desktop publishing software (Adobe PageMaker, Microsoft Publisher, QuarkXPress, Corel Ventura) helps publish documents, magazines and books (like this one). Graphic programs (Adobe Illustrator, CorelDRAW) are used for drawing. Presentation software (Microsoft PowerPoint, Corel Presentations) simplifies developing business presentations to clients and lenders. Project management software (Microsoft Project) helps plan and track complex projects. Contact management software such as ACT! (www.act.com) helps manage business relationships. If you use digital photography (covered later in this chapter) to illustrate your work, consider programs such as Adobe Photoshop to help you manage and enhance your photos.

Other software is also available. You'll learn about them as you enter and explore the world of computer technology, applying what you learn to your love of woodworking.

Using the Internet

So what's all this talk about the "Internet"? And how can the Internet make my woodworking more profitable and enjoyable?

Good questions!

The Internet is an interconnected network of computers that use telephone and other lines to "talk" (share data) with each other. Using hardware called modems (modulator-demodulators), computers dial up other computers (per your instructions), then send and receive data. If the data is in the form called hyper-text markup language (HTML), the results are graphic with formatted text, images and other useful structure. The HTML is read and translated by a browser software program (Netscape Communicator, Microsoft Explorer) and displayed on the computer screen.

Internet Web pages include links, specially formatted words and phrases that, when selected, automatically load another Web page. For example, from the Popular Woodworking Web page (www.popularwoodworking.com), you can select an article title and the link will load the page with the article's text and illustrations.

So what?

Imagine life without telephones. You couldn't call suppliers and order materials, customers couldn't call you to order your products, you couldn't talk with friends. Computers use the telephone and other communication systems in the same way. Using the Internet you can research materials, order supplies, track shipments, show others what your products look like, take orders for your woodworking and even do you banking online.

Certainly you can run your woodworking business without the Internet — and without a telephone. But just as the telephone extends the field of potential customers, so will the Internet. But even if you don't want to mess with photographing your product and setting up a Web site to sell them, you can still use the Internet for research and for buying.

But you don't need to buy a computer and software to get on the Internet. In most communities, libraries or other public resources (colleges, government services) have computers with Internet access for use by the public. If local libraries don't offer access, take a computer or other course at a community college and you can typically use their computer lab. Many communities have Internet cafes or bookstores with Internet access for a small fee. Other communities have copy shops that rent computers. Some large computer stores do the same. Check around!

The Internet has many Web sites for woodworkers, including www.popularwoodworking.com, www.woodworking.com, www.woodweb.com, www.woodworking.org, www.woodworking.about.com, www.woodzone.com, www.womeninwoodworking.com and www.sawdustmaking.com.

You can easily find more using one of the many search engines, including www.google.com, www.yahoo.com and www.dogpile.com. Simply enter a word or phrase in the Search field on these pages and press enter. For example, searching for "woodworking" on Google found more than 2 million sites in 0.15 seconds. Fortunately, they are ranked so the most popular ones are first on the list. Read their search tips to learn how to narrow the search down.

Setting Up Your Web Site

Okay, maybe you've already visited the wonder world of "dub-dub-dub" (www or double-u, double-u, double-u), also known as the Web. And maybe you've decided that you want to sell your woodworking over the Internet. How can you get started?

First, get on the Internet as a consumer. Either through a local library, a friend's computer, one at work or your own, look at the Internet and see

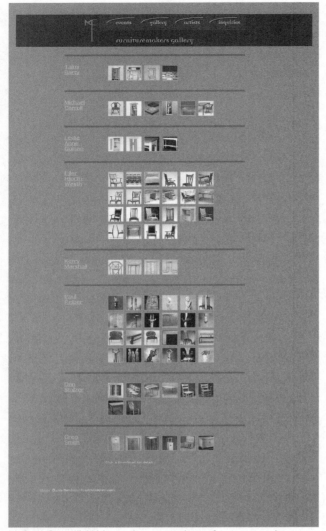

Michael Carroll's Web site (www.mendocinofurniture.com) is just one of many woodworking-related Web sites you will find on the Internet. Above is one page of Michael's Web site.

what it's about. If you have a computer with a modem, you can contact a local or national Internet service provider (ISP). America Online, for example, is a national ISP. Pacific Net is a local ISP that accesses the Internet much as a local telephone service lets you call long distance. The cost varies but is typically $10 to $30 a month plus the computer. Make sure your ISP offers a local access telephone number so you're not paying long-distance charges every time you log on.

You're online. Start looking around for other woodworkers who are already online. You'll quickly learn who's doing what — and how. Keep

notes. Save the URL (uniform resource locator) addresses, such as www.popularwoodworking.com, using the Bookmark feature of your browser software. Figure 6-1 shows a page from (www.mendocinofurniture.com), the Web site for Mendocino Coast Furnituremakers.

Here's some more terminology: The URL www.popularwoodworking.com includes a domain name: popularwoodworking.com. How do you get one of these for yourself? Maybe you want one like superduperwoodcrafter.com. Potential customers can enter your domain name in their browser and quickly access your new Web site from anywhere in the world. Many businesses offer domain name registration. The best place to start is with your ISP. They can check out available names, make suggestions and show you how to "park" your registered domain until you're ready to use it. The fee should be less than $20 a year.

In fact, your ISP probably offers individuals and small businesses a variety of different packages that include Web hosting, storage, e-mail addresses and other services.

How can people buy things over the Internet? Through what are called *secure servers*. A server is a computer that's always on and can be accessed through the Internet. A secure server is one that includes software to encrypt sensitive information such as credit card numbers. It must work because billions of dollars of goods and services are sold over the Internet each year and the fraud level is no more than through traditional businesses.

So whatever ISP you use for selling your woodworking products will require a secure server and related software. Many ISPs offer packages specifically designed for Internet sales. In fact, you can have them or one of their contractors even design your Web site, set up order taking and automatically deposit money in your bank account. Really!

Knowledge is power. Unless you're experienced with Internet buying and selling, either take some time to learn about it or hire someone who already does it. Though hiring a contractor or service is the quickest path, it is also the most expensive. Consider doing it yourself. Excellent books are available on the topic of setting up an Internet site.

An alternative to all this is to link up with other woodworkers in your area or your field and cooperatively market your products on the Internet. It's cheaper than going it alone. But be careful of what you're agreeing to do and pay. Partnerships can make business twice as easy or twice as difficult.

Let's walk through an example (not real) woodworking Web site to see how things happen. The customer uses a search engine (Google, Yahoo, etc.) to search for "marionette." The search returns 520 entries with the word somewhere on the Web site, ranked by density (how many times the word occurs). One of the highest listings is for Mulligan Marionettes, so the customer selects (clicks on) the link, which automatically takes him to www.mulliganmarionettes.com.

Mulligan's Web site includes an introduction, descriptions and photographs of products, a photo and description of the shop, and pricing. The customer selects a Pinocchio marionette at $89.95, and a new Web page appears with the image of a lock at the bottom of the page, indicating a secure page. The customer enters a shipping address and a credit card number and expiration date, then selects "Order."

Behind the scenes, the credit card data is encrypted and sent by a telephone data line to the card authorization company, who reviews it and approves or rejects it within seconds. A "Thank You for Your Order" page appears and the customer goes on his way.

In most cases, an order confirmation is automatically e-mailed to the customer within minutes, confirming product, price and charge. Another automatic e-mail message is typically sent when the product is shipped to the customer.

Want to design and develop your own Web site? You'll need to procure and learn some tools.

Fortunately, it's not that difficult. Web pages are built using a special language called hypertext markup language, or HTML. Many good HTML editors are available for prices ranging from free to $50.00. I like free! The Netscape Navigator browser program (www.netscape.com) includes a composer that lets you build your own Web pages without having to know HTML. Netscape Composer will also let you publish your Web pages by uploading them to your ISP. I'm not a particularly bright guy, and I have built numerous Web sites using these basic tools.

If you'd rather hire someone else to tackle the technology, contact your ISP or a Web sales specialist. Check the local telephone book for Web site developers.

Is a Web site profitable? It depends. The advantage of a Web site for selling your woodworking is that you can now potentially sell to millions of folks who use and buy over the Internet. However, it takes more business and computer skills — and more money — than setting up a table at a craft fair that hundreds visit. So it's not an easy decision to make. But it can be done. Thousands of small businesses, including woodworkers, are setting up profitable businesses on the Internet. So can you!

Setting Up Your E-Mail Account

E-mail is electronic mail. It's probably the major reason why people get on the Internet. With an Internet e-mail account from your ISP and e-mail software (built in to most browser programs), you can send e-mail to customers, friends, suppliers and others around the world. An e-mail address is recognizable as it has an "at" sign — @ — within in. For example, woodworking@danramsey.com is one of my e-mail accounts (I have seven for business, personal and hobby use).

An e-mail account can be ordered from your local ISP or from one of the national ISPs such as America Online (AOL). Free e-mail accounts are available from sources like www.hotmail.com, but typically a string is attached. A one-line advertisement for Hotmail appears at the bottom of every message you send.

Computerized Woodworking Tools

Computers have been at work closer to home, as well. Computer technology has been applied to numerous traditional woodworking tools to make them smarter.

Smarter tools make your work easier and more efficient — which can mean more profitable. They can tackle the mundane jobs, leaving the artistry to you. But more tools mean more cost and maintenance. It's a trade-off.

Computer chips are being built in to table saws, radial-arm saws, drill presses, shapers, planers, band saws and many other large woodworking tools. At minimum, computer chips are behind the digital readouts that can make measurements more accurate. Fractional measurements are accurate to tenths and hundredths of an inch (or the eyesight of the operator), while digital measurements can be accurate to thousandths of an inch or greater. Some machines include computer processors that advise the operator.

Behind the scenes, today's tools are manufactured using more precise measurements and higher tolerances because of computers. This makes them better products and often less expensive through automated machining. And manufacturers using CAD can design better tools faster than traditional blueprinting.

Nowhere has computer technology impacted woodworking more than in measurement. Look at the catalogs and your favorite hardware store for new tools that use technology for accurate measurement. A laser estimator, for example, can precisely measure a distance up to 50' within 3". An elevation measurement system can measure elevations of more than 40' within ⅛". Contractor levels now use lasers to extend plumb and level reference to 100'. Stud sensors today are much more accurate and easy to use than previous models. Measuring tapes now have built-in voice recorders. Handheld calculators can do the math and conversions for thousands of applications.

Traditional woodworking tools are here to stay. But many have received new brains that can help make your projects easier and more accurate.

Other Technology

Computer technology benefits the woodworker in a couple of other fields. The technology is digital.

Compact discs, or CDs, are used to save and view data. The data can be a multimedia training course on using your new radial saw, it can be the entire contents of a book on a single CD, or it can be the music you enjoy while you're working wood. You also can put photos of your best work on CDs and give them to customers to view on their computers.

Multimedia DVDs offer useful information, pictures and video in a portable package. Of course, you'll need a DVD player or DVD reader on your computer to view these disks. Some DVDs train users on tool setup, project ideas and advanced woodworking techniques. They are available from hardware stores and on the Internet.

Another valuable digital technology that woodworkers can use is digital photography. Traditional photography uses light and chemistry to impregnate special paper with images that can be processed into photographs. Digital photography uses light-sensitive components to read an image as digits that can be displayed and printed by a computer.

Besides being fun, digital photography is useful to woodworkers. Digital photographs of your products and processes can be edited on a computer, then printed or uploaded to the Internet. You can take a photograph of your latest project and have it up on the Internet for the world to see within just a few minutes. Amazing!

You'll come up with many applications for digital photography. But you'll need a new tool: a digital camera. They cost from $200 to $1,000 for consumer-level cameras. The quality of a camera is measured by the resolution, or number of dots per inch (dpi). For example, a basic digital camera may have a resolution of 640 × 480 dpi (308 KB), a medium camera of 1600 × 1200 dpi (1.9 MB) and a high-end camera with a resolution of 2272 × 1704 dpi (3.88 MB). Digital cameras are measured by their total resolution. A camera with less than 2 GB is for personal use; above that can be used for professional photography, with the best ones at 4 GB and greater.

If digital photography interests you, start learning about it. Visit computer stores and camera shops to discuss your needs and budget. You can soon learn what's needed to do the job.

Technology has opened many new doors for woodworkers over the past decade. The next decade will be even more exciting!

Do What You Love

Starting to sell your woodworking is somewhat of an experiment. It's an attempt to find out both what you want to make and what others want to buy. And unless you have many years of experience as a woodworker, you probably haven't found exactly what type of woodworking you enjoy most. The message heard from dozens of selling woodworkers is:

1. Find out what you love to do.
2. Find someone who will pay you for doing it.
3. Do it!

As you price your woodworking, you will also evolve as a woodworker. What you make, how you sell it, and your personal and financial goals will all change. You may start out, as many woodworkers do, making anything people want to buy. Slowly, you'll discover what works best for you — and what doesn't. You may determine that you prefer high-production woodworking, making as many fine jewelry boxes as you possibly can. Or you may decide that you want to produce only large hand-carved murals for public display. You search around and find someone who is willing to pay you a fair price for your skills and talents. This may take years of part-time woodworking to discover, during which you want to make sure your prices bring you a profit for your time. Then, possibly during a corporate downsizing, a long-term layoff, early retirement or full retirement, you decide that it's finally time to "do it!"

Your woodworking has been your "escape plan" to help you through frustrating days at the job and to help you afford a better life for you and your family, and has offered you an outlet for your creativity. It may someday become a full-time business for you — or it may not. That's your decision. But along the way, you have enjoyed what you do and helped others through your work. You have contributed to the quality of life for yourself and for others. You have been paid money for it. More important, you have been paid in personal satisfaction. And that's what being a woodworker is all about.

Useful Forms *for* Woodworkers

Materials Use Record

Date

Page _____ of _____

Type of Material:

Location :

Size	Cost	How Used	Amt. Used	Value
			TOTAL	

Notes:

Figure A-1. Master copy of Materials Use Record.

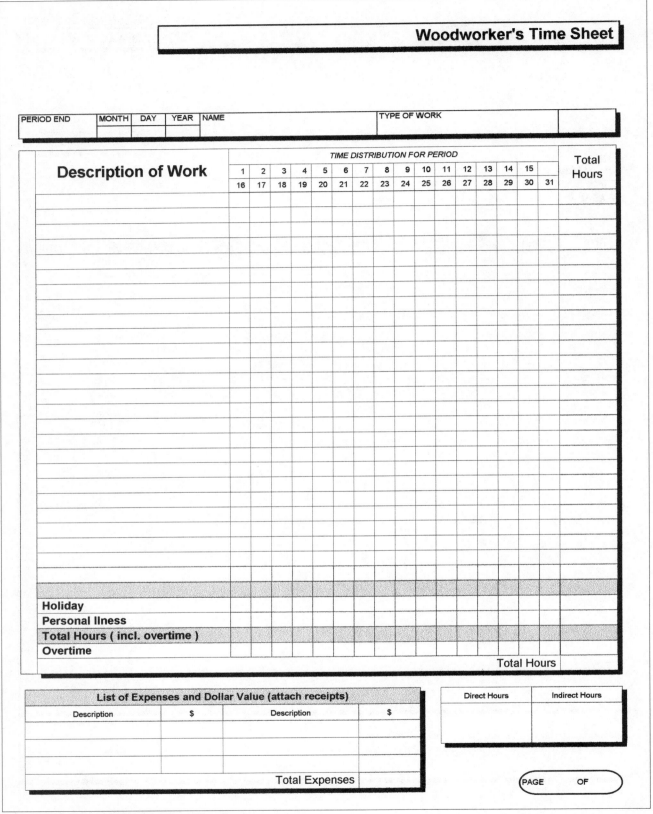

Figure A-2. Master copy of Woodworker's Time Sheet.

Overhead Expenses Estimate

ESTIMATE FOR:

Expense	Rent & Utilities	Equipment & Tools	Supplies	Other Expenses

Figure A-3. Master copy of Overhead Expenses Estimate.

Job Expense Record

DATE

JOB DESCRIPTION AND PROCESS:

MATERIALS

DATE	ITEM	Net Cost	Markup	Total Cost
	Total			

LABOR

DATE	Name	Hours	Rate	Net Cost	Markup	Total Cost
			Total			

CHANGES

DATE	DESCRIPTION	AMOUNT
	Total	

	Net Cost	Markup	Total Cost
Total Materials			
Total Labor			
Total Miscellaneous			
Grand Total			

Figure A-4. Master copy of Job Expense Record.

Features & Benefits Worksheet

Product:

FEATURE What does it have?	BENEFIT Why is it important?

Figure A-5. Master copy of Features & Benefits Worksheet.

Cash Receipts Journal

PERIOD ENDING:

Date	Check Number	Account Number	Amount	Name

Figure A-6. Master copy of Cash Receipts Journal.

Cash Disbursements Journal

PERIOD ENDING:

Date	Check Number	Account Number	Amount	Name

Figure A-7. Master copy of Cash Disbursements Journal.

CREDIT APPLICATION

DATE:

BUSINESS INFORMATION

NAME OF BUSINESS

LEGAL (IF DIFFERENT)

ADDRESS

CITY

STATE	ZIP	PHONE

DESCRIPTION OF BUSINESS

NO. OF EMPLOYEES	CREDIT REQUESTED	TYPE OF BUSINESS

IN BUSINESS SINCE

BUSINESS STRUCTURE

☐ CORPORATION   ☐ PARTNERSHIP   ☐ PROPRIETORSHIP

☐ DIVISION/SUBSIDIARY
NAME OF PARENT
COMPANY _____

HOW LONG IN BUSINESS _____

COMPANY PRINCIPALS RESPONSIBLE FOR BUSINESS TRANSACTIONS

NAME :	TITLE:	ADDRESS:	PHONE:
NAME:	TITLE:	ADDRESS:	PHONE:
NAME:	TITLE:	ADDRESS:	PHONE:

BANK REFERENCES

NAME OF BANK	NAME TO CONTACT
BRANCH	ADDRESS
CHECKING ACCOUNT NO.	TELEPHONE NUMBER

TRADE REFERENCES

FIRM NAME	CONTACT NAME	TELEPHONE NUMBER	ACCOUNT OPEN SINCE

CONFIRMATION OF INFORMATION ACCURACY AND RELEASE OF AUTHORITY TO VERIFY

I hereby certify that the information in this credit application is correct. The information included in this credit application is for use by he above firm in determining the amount and conditions of credit to be extended. I understand that this firm may also utilize the other sources of credit which it considers necessary in making this determination. Further I hereby authorize the bank and trade references listed in this credit application to release the information necessary to assist this firm in establishing a line of credit.

SIGNATURE	TITLE	DATE

POLICY STATEMENT: INITIAL ORDER FROM NEW ACCOUNTS WILL NOT BE PROCESSED UNLESS ACCOMPANIED BY THE ABOVE REQUESTED INFORMATION.
TERMS: NET 30 DAYS FROM DATE OF INVOICE UNLESS OTHERWISE STATED.

Figure A-8. Master copy of Credit Application.

Quotation

Date:

Quote #

Client:

Materials

Quantity	Description	Cost Per Unit	Total
		Total Cost:	

Labor

	Hours	Description	Cost Per Hour	Total
REGULAR				
OVERTIME				
			Total Cost:	

GRAND TOTAL

Authorized Signature   Date

Figure A-9. Master copy of Quotation form.

Shipping

| Trailer/ Car Number | | Bill Date | |

TO

| CONSIGNEE |
| STREET |
| DESTINATION |
| CITY   STATE   ZIP |
| Route: |

FROM

| SHIPPER |
| STREET |
| ORIGIN |
| CITY   STATE   ZIP |
| Special Instructions: |

FOR PAYMENT, SEND BILL TO

| NAME |
| COMPANY |
| STREET |
| CITY   STATE   ZIP |

Shipper's Internal Data

No. Shipping Units	Time	Description of Articles, Special Marks and Exceptions	Weight	Rate	Charges

REMIT C.O.D.
TO:
ADDRESS:
NOTE: Where the rate is dependent on value, shippers are required to state specifically in writing the agreed or declared value of the property. The agreed or declared value of the property is hereby specifically stated by the shipper to be not exceeding
$ _____ per _____

COD AMOUNT: $
If this shipment is to be delivered to the consignee without recourse on the consignor, the consignor shall sign the following statement:
The carrier shall not make delivery of this shipment without payment of freight and all other lawful charges.

_____
(Signature of Consignor)

C.O.D FEE
PREPAID ☐
COLLECT ☐

TOTAL CHARGES $

Freight Charges are collect unless marked prepaid
CHECK BOX IF PREPAID ☐

RECEIVED subject to the classifications and tariffs in effect on the date of the issue of this Bill of Lading, the property described above in apparent good order, except as noted (contents and condition of contents of packages unknown), marked consigned and destined as indicated above which said carrier (the word carrier being understood through this contract as meaning any person or corporation in possession of the property under the contract) agrees to carry to its usual place of delivery as said destination. If on its route, otherwise to deliver to another carrier on the route to said destination. It is mutually agreed as to each carrier of all or any of said property, over all or any portion of said route to destination and as to each party at any time interested in all or any said property, that every service to be performed hereunder shall be subject to all the Bill of Lading terms and conditions in the governing classification on the date of shipment. Shipper hereby certifies that he is familiar with all the Bill of Lading terms and conditions in the governing classification and the said terms and conditions are hereby agreed to by the shipper and accepted for himself and his assigns.

| Shipper | Carrier | |
| Per | Per | Date: |

Figure A-10. Master copy of Shipping form.

Cash Flow Forecast

DATE:

FOR TIME PERIOD:

APPROVED BY:

PREPARED BY:

FOR INTERNAL USE ONLY

	Date:		Date:		Date:	
	ESTIMATE	ACTUAL	ESTIMATE	ACTUAL	ESTIMATE	ACTUAL
Opening Balance						
Collections From Trade						
Misc. Cash Receipts						
TOTAL CASH AVAILABLE						
DISBURSEMENTS						
Payroll						
Trade Payables						
Other						
Capital Expenses						
Income Tax						
Bank Loan Payment						
TOTAL DISBURSEMENTS						
Ending Balance						
Less Minimum Balance						
CASH AVAILABLE						

Figure A-11. Master copy of Cash Flow Forecast.

Price List

Date:

Product	Description	Price

Figure A-12. Master copy of Price List form.

Monthly Activity Planner

PERSON:

FROM:

TO:

PRIORITIES	Monday	Tuesday	Wednesday	Thursday	Friday	Saturday	Sunday
1							
2							
3							
4							
5							

Figure A-13. Master copy of Monthly Activity Planner.

Project Planner

Project:

1 _____ ⬭

2 _____ ⬭

3 _____ ⬭

4 _____ ⬭

5 _____ ⬭

6 _____ ⬭

7 _____ ⬭

8 _____ ⬭

9 _____ ⬭

10 _____ ⬭

11 _____ ⬭

12 _____ ⬭

Figure A-14. Master copy of Project Planner.

Index

More Great Books from Popular Woodworking Books!

Learn the mechanics of getting your ideas down on paper and refining them into construction drawings and cutting lists. You'll learn to create a drawing from a photo, resize furniture plans with easy formulas, standard furniture dimensions and much more!

DESIGN YOUR OWN FURNITURE
by Jim Stack
ISBN 1-55870-613-5, paperback,
128 pages, #70555-K

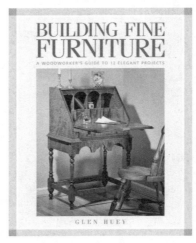

You'll see traditional joinery, modern methods, finishing secrets and techniques that will make you a better woodworker. And, you'll discover the plans, tricks and techniques Huey used to construct 12 pieces of well-built, well-proportioned furniture that almost anyone would be pleased to have in their home.

BUILDING FINE FURNITURE
by Glen Huey
ISBN 1-55870-645-3, paperback,
128 pages, #70593-K

This book is a collection of the 23 best projects in the Arts & Crafts style that have appeared in *Popular Woodworking* magazine during the last four years. Each project comes with a complete cutting list, construction drawings and photos of each step of the process.

AUTHENTIC ARTS & CRAFTS FURNITURE PROJECTS
by the Editors of *Popular Woodworking* Magazine
ISBN 1-55870-568-6, paperback,
128 pages, #70499-K

You'll get complete plans for 10 pieces of truly excellent Shaker furniture that are built with a low budget of tools but with high demands for quality. The casework featured runs the entire gamut of complexity. Start with the simple 1840 wall clock that is assembled with a minimum of joints. Move on to a simple dovetailed cupboard that will allow you to practice this traditional skill without demanding months of slaving over a large case.

AUTHENTIC SHAKER FURNITURE
by Kerry Pierce
ISBN 1-55870-657-7, paperback,
128 pages, #70607-K

These and other great woodworking books are available at your local bookstore, woodworking stores, online suppliers or by calling 1-800-448-0915. When calling please use savings code TBA05PWB.